AT HOME WITH
BEATRIX POTTER

THE CREATOR OF PETER RABBIT

AT HOME WITH
BEATRIX POTTER

THE CREATOR OF PETER RABBIT

SUSAN DENYER

HARRY N. ABRAMS, INC., PUBLISHERS

Library of Congress Cataloging-in-Publication Data

Denyer, Susan.
    At home with Beatrix Potter/Susan Denyer.
      p.cm.
    Includes bibliographical references (p.)
    and index.
    ISBN 0-8109-4112-0 (cloth)/
    0-8109-2106-5 (pbk)
    1. Potter, Beatrix. 1866-1943—Homes and
haunts—England—Lake District. 2. Women
conservationists—England—Lake District—
Biography. 3. Women authors, English—20th century—Biography. 4. Women artists—Great Britain—
Biography. 5. Lake District (England)—Biography.
6. Children's stories—Illustrations.
7. Children's stories—Authorship. I. Title.

PR6031.O72 Z585 2000
823'.912—dc21
[B]   99-44929

Printed and bound in China
10 9 8 7 6 5 4 3 2 1

Harry N. Abrams, Inc.
100 Fifth Avenue
New York, N.Y. 10011
www.abramsbooks.com

Abrams is a subsidiary of

LA MARTINIÈRE
G R O U P E

*This book is dedicated to
the past, present and future tenants
of Beatrix Potter's farms*

PAGE 1 *Looking from the parlour into the hall at Hill Top.*

PAGES 2-3 *Watercolour sketch, c. 1905, by Beatrix Potter of Hill Top Farm, Near Sawrey, looking across Esthwaite Water towards the Langdale Pikes. She found Sawrey to be 'very pretty hilly country, but not wild like Keswick or Ullswater . . .'*

ABOVE *One of the last photographs of Beatrix, standing with her cat by the vegetable garden gate at Hill Top.*

RIGHT *Beatrix's paintbox, inscribed with her mother's name Helen Leech.*

CONTENTS

FAMILY AND HOLIDAY HOMES

ABOVE *Beatrix painted this view from the nursery window of 2 Bolton Gardens, the Potters' London home, in June 1882, a month before she first visited the Lake District. The Potters had moved into the newly built house the year Beatrix was born. In the distance is the tower of the Natural History Museum.*

RIGHT *The Potter family with their dog, Spot, photographed by Beatrix's father, Rupert Potter, on the right, outside Wray Castle, overlooking Windermere in 1882. The castle was built in 1845 by James Dawson, a Liverpool surgeon, with, Beatrix said, 'his wife's money . . . her father Robert Preston made gin; that was where the money came from . . . it took seven years to finish. The stone was brought across the lake. One old horse dragged it all up to the house on a kind of tram way.'*

IN 1905 BEATRIX POTTER bought Hill Top Farm at Near Sawrey in the Lake District. The purchase heralded the beginning of a remarkable partnership between Beatrix Potter, artist and storyteller, and her adopted home. By the time of her death almost forty years later she had built up an estate of 4,000 acres of the central Lake District, and had become an exceedingly effective protagonist for preserving its vulnerable farming culture. For the last twenty years of her life, Beatrix Potter was better known as Mrs William Heelis, farmer, sheep-breeder and staunch supporter of the Lake District countryside.

In 1925, Beatrix was asked by the editor of *The Horn*, a magazine produced by the Boston Bookshop, to write a few words about herself for her many admirers in America. She wrote: 'Beatrix Potter is Mrs William Heelis. She lives in the north of England, her home is amongst the mountains and lakes that she has drawn in her picture books. Her husband is a lawyer. They have no family. Mrs Heelis is in her 60th year. She leads a very busy contented life, living always in the country and managing a large sheep farm on her own land.' In a letter accompanying these words, she also added: 'I don't think anybody requires to know more about me.'

Nevertheless she did write a few words more to explain how and why she began writing *The Tale of Peter Rabbit*, the first of her now world-famous picture books. 'I used to write picture letters to a little invalid boy years and years ago, the eldest child of a friend.

ABOVE *Beatrix aged five, holding a toy rabbit. She is with her cousin Alice Crompton Potter.*

OPPOSITE *Drawings of twelve caterpillars from a sketchbook Beatrix filled during a holiday at Dalguise, Perthshire, when she was nine years old. On the following page she noted the habits of some of her specimens: 'The caterpillar is dark brown with orange dots. I don't know what it eats, but I think it is the flowering nettle. It is found by hedges in May and June. Bombycidal.'*

Peter was written to him in a letter ... About 1900 there began to be a fashion for little picture books, and I thought Peter might be worthwhile publishing. But I could not find anyone else who thought so. It was refused by many publishers, and I got a small number printed for myself with pen and ink illustrations like the scribbles in the original letter. That is the history of Peter Rabbit. I have never been able to understand what is the attraction of the book but it continues to sell.'

Beatrix was born in London in 1866. She lived with her parents, Rupert and Helen Potter, in Bolton Gardens, South Kensington, for forty-seven years before moving north to settle in the Lake District. The Potters were prosperous. Both sides of the family had earned substantial fortunes from textiles, her paternal grandparents in Derbyshire and her maternal grandparents in Lancashire. Rupert had been called to the bar but did not practise as a barrister; instead he led a social life, mixing with some of the eminent politicians, writers, artists and photographers of his day.

From her earliest childhood, Beatrix was to become an acute observer of houses and the countryside. Every year the family vacated their house for two weeks in the spring, and during August and September took longer holidays. Beatrix also visited her relations around the country. During all these visits she noted, sketched and distilled the essence of her favourite rooms and spaces, and meticulously recorded plants, fossils and animals.

Caterpillars.

One of the first family houses to make its imprint on Beatrix was Camfield Place, the home of her grandparents, Edmund and Jessie Potter. The year she was born, her grandfather had retired from running his calico printing works at Glossop, in Derbyshire, and moved to Camfield Place near Hatfield in Hertfordshire. The place 'I love best in the world', as she described it, was, when her grandfather bought it, 'a good-sized small-roomed old house of no particular pretensions, the outside, red-brick, whitewashed'. It was set in a 300-acre estate with 'trees in every hedge row . . . the distant sounds of the farmyard' and in the summer 'the all pervading smell of new mown hay'. Edmund had pulled down part of the house and built a large addition in yellow terracotta bricks. It was the earlier part that appealed to Beatrix: 'I have always liked the old part of the house best', she wrote; 'the new rooms are not bad in taste . . . but they are rather uncomfortably large.'

Her affections were engaged most strongly in the 'below-stairs' part of the house, the powerhouse of the domestic arrangements. This was the realm of 'Nanny Netticoat', a little old lady with white woollen stockings, black velvet slippers and a mob-cap. Here Beatrix relished all the details: 'the large scullery with a stone oven and a great vat for making broth, also a curious smoke jack in the chimney, and a plague of another sort of jacks which are black [?jackdaws]'; the linen room with its 'doors opening in the panels without rhyme or reason . . . and sunlight dimples on the whitewashed ceiling'.

During her visits, Beatrix always slept in bedroom number four and she had the use of the day nursery. She later remembered vividly in the day room the drugget (a protective covering for the carpet), tightly stretched, a rocking chair and a work box, 'banished for its old fashioned ugliness', and in the bedroom 'the bedstead with green hangings' with its hollow brass pole (which she once took down to extract a tame dormouse), 'the chairs, the looking glass and 8 pictures, also the alabaster figure of Ariadne riding the leopard, which was under the glass shade on the mantelpiece'. The bedroom furnishings were so special for her that she asked for, and was given them, after Jessie Potter died in 1891, when Camfield Place was sold.

Her grandmother's death prompted reflection on the intensely happy times Beatrix had spent in the house, and she wrote a short essay, 'Memories of Camfield Place', to an imaginary correspondent called Esther. Camfield was Beatrix's Blakesmoor: just as the essayist and poet Charles Lamb had been provided with memories he never forgot by the country house, Blakesware, in which his grandmother had been a housekeeper (and which he wrote about as Blakesmoor), so too had Camfield developed in Beatrix

intense feelings for old spaces, well-groomed countryside, the feeling of plenty and the satisfaction of what she saw as a 'perfect whole'.

In the essay, Beatrix reflected on how her artistic perceptions had sharpened during the time she knew Camfield Place: 'What a great deal we lose in growing wise!' she wrote. In getting older (and she was still only twenty-four) she had begun to realize the shortcomings of the nursery furnishings. Paintings which to a child had seemed to be awe-inspiring alpine scenes turned now to daubs of paint; and the plaster-of-Paris busts, 'which had seemed almost real people in the twilight', now, even allowing for the over-enthusiastic cleaning of the maid, Zipperah, no longer radiated elegance. 'Sir Walter Raleigh is a stick', she wrote, and 'the lady who leans on a rock in a corner above the hot-water pipes is absurdly too tall; she used to be my ideal of elegance'.

Her other grandmother, Jane Leech, lived at Gorse Hall, near Stalybridge, also on the edge of the Pennines. Both sides of the family had originally come from near Manchester, where their fortunes had been made in cotton. As she put it: 'our descent – our interests and our joy was in the north country'.

Beatrix visited Gorse Hall less frequently than Camfield Place. After Jane Leech's death in 1884, when Beatrix was eighteen, she paid her last visit there. Before arriving she was full of apprehension: 'I have very pleasant recollections of it, which I fear may have changed. I have now seen longer passages and higher halls . . . the passage I used to patter along so kindly on the way to bed will no longer seem dark and mysterious . . . It is six or seven years since I have been there, but I remember it like yesterday. The pattern of the doormat, the pictures on the old music-box, the sound of the rocking horse as it swung, the engraving on the stair, the smell of the Indian corn, and the feeling of plunging ones hands into the bin, the hooting of the turkeys and the quick flutter of the fantails' wings. I would not have it changed.'

But changed it was: 'My first feeling on entering the door was regret that I had come. How small the hall had grown and – there was a new doormat, but in a minute or two it had come back. It was the same old place, the same quiet light and the same smell – I wonder why houses smell so different. On thinking of a place the first recollection is the smell and amount of light.' She helped her mother and Aunt Harriet, her mother's sister, clear out the house and divide the valuables – 'a scene . . . at once so ridiculous and melancholy that I shall never forget it'. She was pained at the way scant regard was given to any associations the remaining contents may have had – they could not reach Grandpapa's wedding clothes on top of a cupboard and she noted 'it is extraordinary how little people value old things if they are of little intrinsic value'.

LEFT *A corner of the library at Wray Castle, overlooking Windermere, sketched by Beatrix in July 1882, during the three and a half months the Potters were on holiday there. Several friends came to stay, such as William Gaskell, the Unitarian minister and widower of Mrs Gaskell the novelist, and John Bright, the Quaker politician and orator who had just resigned from the Cabinet. They also entertained the local vicar, the Revd Hardwicke Rawnsley (later Canon Rawnsley), whose church was at the end of the castle drive.*

OPPOSITE *Two views of the hall at Gwaynynog, Denbigh, painted by Beatrix (the painting on the right is dated 1904; the date for the view on the left is unknown). The tall three-storey oak cupboard, which she called 'a Welsh dresser, date 1696', was probably part of the oak furniture bought with the house by her uncle, Fred Burton. This room was to influence the way Beatrix laid out and furnished the hall at Hill Top.*

A few years later, Aunt Harriet and her husband Fred Burton moved from Manchester to Denbigh, in north Wales. In 1895 Beatrix made her first visit to them at Gwaynynog, the ancestral home of the Myddletons, cousins of the Myddletons of Chirk Castle. The older part of the house was timber-framed, dating from the 1570s, with an early nineteenth-century stone front 'unhappily refaced with sham gothic'. Fred's elder brother Oliver Burton had bought the house from the Myddletons who were, as Beatrix put it, through 'lavish prodigality ... reduced to living in the kitchen'.

While she had remembered and relished Camfield Park and Gorse Hall for their associations with happy childhood times, Beatrix was older, more dispassionate when she first visited Gwaynynog and the house appealed to her for what she saw as its 'perfect taste'. Uncle Fred had spent his considerable cotton fortune refurbishing the place, embellishing his decoration with the Burton family crest — a hand grasping a cotton plant. When the Burtons arrived in the house there were fine chimneypieces, a panelled room and apparently a good deal of oak furniture. To all of this Uncle Fred added a 'truly wonderful collection of Chippendale mahogany'. Beatrix wrote: 'I have never seen rooms more faultless in scheme of colour or Sheraton more elegant without being flimsy.' Over the fifteen years she visited the house she did numerous sketches and water-colours of its smaller rooms and older spaces, but not of the grandly furnished sitting rooms: just as with Camfield Place, Beatrix felt more in tune with the earlier part of the house and she frequently sketched the hall with its old oak.

Family holidays during the first thirty years of her life also provided a source of material for Beatrix's interest in the shapes and forms of household spaces. Each year the Potter family left London at spring-cleaning time, often for the West Country, and stayed in hotels, from which they made forays to other towns. In the summer they also had a lengthy stay of up to three months in a large country house rented for the duration. For the first eighteen years it was mostly in Scotland, eleven of those at Dalguise House at Dunkeld. Then from 1882 they spent several summers in the Lake District, where they rented first Wray Castle on Windermere, and in later years other houses such as Lingholm on Derwentwater.

As she travelled Beatrix sketched: old houses at Winchelsea on the coast in Sussex, a house at Skelghyll near Gutherscale in the Lake District, mill buildings at Dalguise House in Tayside, the store passages at Bedwell Lodge, near Hatfield, Hertfordshire. What fascinated her were the haphazard arrangements of farm buildings, changes in level in the rambling back passages of large houses, shafts of light through doors and the warm glow of fires from cavernous fireplaces. These were her recurring themes.

On one holiday with her parents when she was eighteen, she visited an antiques shop in Oxford 'filled with furniture, china and every kind of old curiosity'. Amongst the twenty or thirty pieces of old oak she saw was a cupboard similar to one at Wray Castle which she admired particularly and wished to possess. She wrote: 'if I ever had a house I would have old furniture, oak in the dining room and Chippendale

in the drawing room. It is not as expensive as modern furniture and incomparably handsomer and better made.'

These holidays also gave Beatrix a love for and empathy with the countryside that remained throughout her life. When the family's stays at Dalguise came to an end she looked back at the way the landscape there had fed her romantic imagination. 'The woods were peopled by the mysterious good folk ... half believing the superstitions of the district, seeing my own fancies so clearly that they become true to me, I lived in a separate world,' she wrote. As the great harvest moon rose over the hills, 'the fairies came out to dance on the smooth turf, the night-jar's eerie cry was heard, the hooting of the owls, the bat flitted round the house, roe-deer's bark sounded from the dark woods, and faint in the distance, then nearer and nearer came the strange world music of the summer breeze'.

The years of Lake District holidays coincided with Beatrix, who seems never to have been a particularly fit or healthy child, becoming stronger physically, as well as more confident and more of an observer of the real world. 'It is nearly as perfect a little place as I ever lived in, and such nice

OVERLEAF *Hawkshead, seen looking towards Latterbarrow and Claife Heights. Beatrix first visited Hawkshead in August 1882, walking from Wray Castle along the footpaths. 'Went to Hawkshead on 19th. Had a series of adventures. Inquired the way three times, lost continually, alarmed by collies at every farm, stuck in stiles, chased once by cows.'*

old-fashioned people in the village,' she wrote of Near Sawrey in 1896. Reflecting on this change in her perceptions when she returned to London in the autumn, she wrote: 'I remember I used to half believe and wholly play with fairies when I was a child. What heaven can be more real than to retain the spirit-world of child-hood, tempered and balanced by knowledge and common-sense, to fear no longer the terror that flieth by night, yet to feel truly and understand a little, a very little, of the story of life.'

She spent her Lake District days sketching and searching for fossils and fungi. She drove her gig around the lanes and the old lady, as she called her horse, 'took the corners in great style. I like a road where one can spin along.' She kept in touch with a wide network of people, such as the staff at Wray Castle, and the Faucits at Tock Howe Farm, Wray. Her journals at this time reflect a mixture of detachment, acute observation and analysis of the natural world, increasing interest in people and their ways, and yet all still spiced with a wish to see beyond the immediate reality.

She wrote short, pithy pen-portraits of many of those she met: the lady at the gate of an old-fashioned house near Hawkshead, 'the most funniest old lady, large black cap, spectacles, apron, ringlets, a tall new rake much higher than herself and apparently no legs: she had stepped out of a fairy tale'; Polly who 'sortied in a brown cloak and a hat with two defiant feathers . . .' out from Limefitt Farm, Troutbeck; Mrs Hanes and her 'caats' (cats in the local dialect) in an old row of cottages above Sky Hill in Coniston 'with black hair and eyes, in spectacles, with a clean cottage and soapy hands . . . gesticulating in the middle of her flagged kitchen'; blind Billy Hamilton who 'went about with a wheel-barrow collecting sticks, entering thickets with the immunity of the men of Thessaly' to supply wood chips for the stove in Coniston Church.

She relished the fullness of the autumn harvest at Wray Castle, where 'down in the scullery of the great kitchen Jane had a clothes-basket full of elder-berries for wine, some greeney-white, a variety I never saw. She had already made damson wine and ginger, and outside was a litter of walnuts blown down by the gale. It is a season for wild fruits, haws on the bushes as red-over as red hawthorn in spring, crabs and wild bullaces, little sound amber plums, and blackberries, more than I ever saw except at Coniston. It is a kindly berry, it ripens in the rain.' Above Near Sawrey she came across a remote 'hennery whence proceeded singular thumpings and bumpings' and discovered after making a 'circum valley observation, with suspicion of mills or gypsies, and the assistance of sheep' that it was caused by 'two nasty broody old hens shut up in a barrel'.

On her thirtieth birthday Beatrix wrote how she felt younger and stronger than at twenty, both in mind and body. But her belief in the other world, or her wish to have such a belief, had not left her. That same year in London she recalled one of the most pleasant memories of her summer. Sitting on a table of rock on Oatmeal Crag, above Near Sawrey, one Sunday afternoon, she could survey 'all the little tiny fungus people singing and bobbing and dancing in the grass and under the leaves all down below, like the whistling that some people cannot hear of stray mice and bats, and I sitting up above knowing something about them. I cannot tell what possesses me with the fancy that they laugh and clap their hands, especially the little ones that grow in troops and rings amongst dead leaves in the woods. I suppose it is the fairy rings, the myriads of fairy fungi that start into life in autumn woods.'

Her unashamed imagination combined with an ability to craft words and above all create pictures was beginning to provide her with a degree of independence. In 1890, encouraged by her uncle, Sir Henry Roscoe, she had offered six designs of rabbits, dressed up in clothes, based on her pet rabbit, Benjamin Bouncer, to the publishers Hildesheimer and Faulkner, then the leading card producers. They bought them immediately for £6 to use as Christmas cards. Beatrix did not invent the anthropomorphic Christmas card; Christmas cards had first been produced commercially in 1846, and by 1890 animals dressed as humans had become the most popular subject depicted on them. Beatrix invested her subjects with an extraordinary dynamic intensity, based on years of study of animals and her ability to compose pictures with a wonderfully tight focus, elevating her designs to the status of paintings.

The rabbit drawings were followed by others of mice and guinea-pigs, and these were also published as cards by Hildesheimer and Faulkner. She produced a set of pictures entitled *The Rabbits' Christmas Party* and also illustrations of nursery rhymes such as 'Three little mice sat down to spin'. Many years later she appended a note to some copies of the Christmas cards, bundled up at Hill Top — 'designs sold to Hildesheimer & Faulkner a German firm in London possibly in 90's or 80's. First thing that was published. I never liked the cards.'

FAMILY AND HOLIDAY HOMES

OPPOSITE *Beatrix with her pet rabbit, Benjamin Bouncer, in September 1891, photographed by Rupert Potter. She bought him from 'a London bird shop in a paper bag. His existence was not observed . . . for a week.' When on holiday in Perthshire she wrote how she used to 'walk him about with a leather strap. He is the object of many odd comments . . .'*

LEFT *Sketches, made around 1890, of Benjamin Bouncer, whom Beatrix used as a model for designs she made for Christmas cards.*

BELOW *One of the first Christmas cards Beatrix had published by Hildesheimer and Faulkner in 1890. It is entitled 'A Happy Pair' and signed H.B.P. 'What an investment that rabbit has been,' she said, 'in spite of the hutches.' To celebrate her success in selling her first drawings, she fed Benjamin hemp seeds with the result that next morning he was 'partially intoxicated and wholly unmanageable'.*

Eastwood Dunkeld
Sep 4th 93

My dear Noel,
       I don't know what to
write to you, so I shall tell you a story
about four little rabbits
                  whose names were.

Flopsy, Mopsy, Cottontail

and Peter

They lived with their mother in a
sand bank under the root of a
big fir tree.

LEFT *By 1893 Beatrix had a pet rabbit called Peter. He travelled to Scotland with the family for the summer of 1893 when they stayed at Eastwood near Dunkeld on the River Tay. It was there that Beatrix penned her now-famous letter about Peter to Noel, the young son of Annie Moore.*

OPPOSITE ABOVE *Beatrix with Canon Rawnsley outside Ghyll Head, near Windermere, in 1912. Rawnsley helped Beatrix find a publisher for her story of Peter Rabbit, even going so far as to adapt her text by turning it into rhyming doggerel. Frederick Warne, the publishers, wrote to Rawnsley to say they would take the book but did not like his verses, preferring instead to reinstate Beatrix's simple narrative.*

OPPOSITE BELOW *The manuscript of* The Tale of Peter Rabbit, *written in a lined exercise book with the illustrations slotted in. The privately printed edition of* Peter Rabbit *was published on 16 December 1901. Beatrix gave away some of the 250 copies as Christmas presents and sold the remainder for 1s each, plus 2d for postage.*

In 1893 Beatrix wrote from Scotland to Noel, the young son of Annie Moore, her one-time governess. Because he was unwell, she decided to illustrate the letter. This picture letter proved to be a defining moment for Beatrix. 'My dear Noel,' she wrote, 'I don't know what to write to you, so I shall tell you a story about four little rabbits whose names were Flopsy, Mopsy, Cottontail and Peter.' More picture letters followed to other Moore children – there were five – and all were kept and treasured by the recipients. In 1900 Annie Moore suggested to Beatrix that the stories she had written would make good books. Beatrix sought the advice of Canon Rawnsley, who had written and published poems for children. She had met Rawnsley when she was sixteen while staying with her parents at Wray Castle. He was then vicar of Wray, his church at the end of the castle drive. The meeting marked the beginning of a friendship and a mutual admiration that lasted until Rawnsley's death in 1921.

Beatrix developed a story of Peter Rabbit from her first picture letter and, with Rawnsley's help, approached several publishers. All turned down her manuscript and so she decided to publish the book privately. It proved to be an instant success, with all 250 copies being sold in the first two weeks or so. Almost immediately the publishers Frederick Warne agreed to produce commercially a coloured version. It went on sale in 1902, and 8,000 copies were ordered before publication. Beatrix had begun her career as storyteller and artist.

and tried to put his foot upon Peter, who jumped out of a window upsetting three plants. The window was too small for Mr McGregor, and he was tired of pursuing Peter. He went back to his work.

By 1905 she had written six 'little books', as they came to be known: *The Tales of Peter Rabbit, Squirrel Nutkin, Benjamin Bunny, Two Bad Mice, The Pie and The Patty-Pan* and *The Tailor of Gloucester.* At the same time, she had continued to produce dozens of other drawings. When, for instance, the family had stayed near Keswick in the years between 1897 and 1899, Beatrix filled her sketch books with drawings of the Lake District and two of her stories are obviously set there — *Benjamin Bunny*

in the garden at Fawe Park and *Squirrel Nutkin* on the shores of Derwentwater. She also distilled images from real life and transposed them into different settings. Favourite spaces from her childhood became elements in the mythical landscapes and roomscapes inhabited by her animal characters. Again and again in her drawings we find the essence of the rooms she loved as a child — the focal fires, the grandfather clock, oak furniture, narrow passages, changes of level and shafts of light. Fragments of houses which had shielded and protected her are now peopled by her characters: Peter Rabbit's burrow is warmed by the glow of the fire, and mice are shown in the store room passage at Camfield Place, seated spinning on the Camfield bentwood chairs or sheltered by the all-enveloping hangings of her grandmother's bed.

Without a house of her own, Beatrix had to confine her domestic feelings to sketches and drawings in which she created wonderful, imaginary interiors. These interiors are simultaneously practical, magical and quint-essentially English, possessing the power to cocoon their inhabitants against the terrors of the wider world.

LEFT *View across Derwentwater. Beatrix filled sketchbooks with views of Derwentwater and the Newlands valley, to the west of the lake, when she was staying at Lingholm for the summers of 1897 to 1899. It was at Lingholm that she continued her friendship with Rawnsley, who was by now Vicar of Crosthwaite on the outskirts of Keswick.*

RIGHT *View of the Newlands valley. Beatrix used her sketches of the Newlands valley, and in particular ones of a cottage in Little Town, as inspiration for a story about a hedgehog called Mrs. Tiggy-Winkle. Lucie Carr, one of the daughters of the vicar of Newlands, became Lucie in the book.*

FURNISHING HILL TOP

LEFT *Beatrix's clogs and one of her spinning wheels next to the fire in the hall at Hill Top. Beatrix took to wearing wooden-soled clogs when she became a farmer. She wore them almost to the exclusion of anything else, even at sheep shows, although local farmers preferred to wear shoes or boots to such events.*

BELOW *One of Beatrix's fantasy interiors. This is part of a set of illustrations for a nursery rhyme, 'Three Little Mice Sat Down to Spin' c. 1892. The mice are shown seated on bentwood and cane chairs. The model for these, a chair from bedroom number four at Camfield Place, is now in the new room at Hill Top.*

BY 1905 THE 'LITTLE BOOKS' had been outstandingly successful and Beatrix had earned enough money to consider acquiring a place of her own. She decided to look for a small farm in the Lake District. Since her first visit to Near Sawrey when staying at Wray Castle in 1882, she had got to know the area much better during family holidays at Lakefield, a large house with gardens overlooking Esthwaite Water. The Potters went there first in 1896 and again in 1900, by which time the house had been renamed Ees Wyke ('house on the shore').

Apparently Beatrix mentioned to one of the servants at Ees Wyke that she would like to acquire a small farm in Near Sawrey and was told in 1905 that Hill Top Farm could be for sale. It had already changed hands twice that year when it was offered to Beatrix: it had been bought first by a timber dealer in May with 151 acres

who then sold it on with 34 acres to a local landowner the following September; the landowner heard of Beatrix's interest and offered it to her but at more than double the price he had paid. The residents of Near Sawrey may have seemed quaint and old-fashioned but they could see a profitable deal on the horizon. Beatrix bought the farm in November for £2,805, using the money from her little books together with a small legacy. She may not have been that financially astute in her first purchase, but she was to make up for it in her property deals later in life. The villagers were somewhat bemused by their new neighbour: 'My purchase seems to be regarded as a huge joke.'

When Beatrix became its owner, Hill Top Farm was being managed by John Cannon, who lived there with his wife. She considered asking him to leave but then

LEFT *Beatrix sketched this view from just outside the garden at Ees Wyke looking towards Esthwaite Water in June 1911. The small building rising up from the garden wall is a two-storey summer house. Such buildings are quite a feature of gardens in Kendal and the south of the Lake District.*

RIGHT *From the back of the farm buildings at Hill Top there are views over the south end of Esthwaite Water. Beatrix sketched the lake on numerous occasions, recording all its moods and seasons. 'I prefer a pastoral landscape backed by mountains,' she said, adding, 'I have often been laughed at for thinking Esthwaite Water the most beautiful of the Lakes.'*

realized that there were many advantages in having him run things for her, and so she asked him to stay.

Her ownership of the farm brought her some solace from deep personal grief. Earlier in the summer, after a friendship of five years, Norman Warne, a member of the Warne family of publishers who had greatly supported Beatrix in the development and publication of her stories, had proposed to her and been accepted. The engagement lasted only a month before Norman died from a rapid form of leukaemia. Even before the farm deal was signed and sealed Beatrix was paying lengthy visits to the property and finding a welcome respite from her sad loss in the day-to-day routines of farm life. 'The pigs are sold — at what drapers call a "sacrifice"; . . . the whole district is planted out with my pigs; but we still take an interest in them because if they grow well we shall "get a name for pigs". Such is fame!' Harold Warne, her publisher and Norman's brother, was soon regaled with farm vignettes: 'the last ill-luck is that a rat has taken *ten* fine turkey eggs last night. The silly hen was sitting calmly on nothing, Mr S Whiskers having tunnelled underneath the coop, and removed the eggs down the hole!'

Beatrix still had commitments in London: her mother refused to allow her to forsake helping her with domestic arrangements on a regular basis and so for the first few years of her ownership Beatrix could visit Hill Top only as often as her obligations would allow. She travelled up and down by train and stayed in Near Sawrey with the Satterthwaites, the blacksmith and his wife, at Belle Green in Smithy Lane, until alterations had been carried out to the house.

LEFT *Hill Top, photographed by Beatrix in 1902, three years before she bought the farm. In the doorway are Mrs Preston, the wife of the then tenant, and Mrs Beckett, the wife of Beatrix's mother's coachman, who lodged at Hill Top while the family stayed at Ees Wyke. The little boy is David Beckett, who was born in 1900.*

The house at Hill Top is a small Lake District farmhouse dating back to the late seventeenth century. It was altered and enlarged in the eighteenth century, when a handsome staircase wing was added, and again in the nineteenth century, when it was given sash windows and a slate porch. The house is constructed of local slate and, when Beatrix bought it, it was rendered on the outside with pebbly lime mortar, whitened with a thin coat of limewash. As with so many Lake District houses, the plainness and almost severity of the exterior contrasts strongly with the richness of the interior.

The heart of Lake District farmhouses is the room known variously as the firehouse, the house-place or sometimes simply the house. In the seventeenth century this was often the only heated room and the one where cooking and eating took place. It was also the main circulation space: the entrance door opened into the firehouse and to get to the rest of the rooms you had to pass through it. The other main rooms on the ground floor were the parlour, which until the early nineteenth century in many houses still functioned as the main bedroom, and the larder or buttery for keeping food and utensils. Sometimes houses had a second heated room downstairs, known as the kitchen or downhouse, where brewing and baking took place. Upstairs, until late into the nineteenth century, the rooms were often unceiled and used not only for sleeping but also for storing grain and other produce such as apples.

Across the Lake District there are strong similarities in house-building traditions but also quite marked differences between valleys. These differences concern not only the size of the buildings but also the way the ground-floor rooms and the stairs relate to the main firehouse. Hill Top is modest in size and in its seventeenth-century layout had a compact plan, with a buttery and parlour opening off the firehouse and a small spiral staircase tucked into one side of the fireplace. It has none of the pretensions of some of the much larger farmhouses which can be found in neighbouring Hawkshead and Coniston – houses that Beatrix was to own herself later in life.

When Beatrix bought Hill Top, its seventeenth-century core had been extended. At the rear, a staircase wing and adjoining larder had been added, and on the farmyard side, a one-storey kitchen. Within a few months of her purchase she had put in hand plans to enlarge the house further to make two living spaces: the old farmhouse for herself and a new wing for the Cannons, to be created by replacing the one-storey kitchen with an enlarged two-storey wing. This was her first essay in building design and she based her sketches on detailed observations of Lake District buildings. Surviving sketches show how her thoughts emerged on the best way to tackle the new roof – whether to have a gable facing the front, or alternatively to have the new ridge in line with the old one. Once the plans were finalized, she hired local craftsmen for the building work. Supervising their progress was not without problems. 'I had rather a row with the plumber, or perhaps I ought to say I lost my temper! The men have been very good so far; if he wont take orders from a lady, I may pack him off and get one from Kendal.'

By the end of 1906 the new wing was finished, with a pentice roof (or canopy) sheltering the front door beneath a plaque bearing Beatrix's initials and the date. The wing and the old house had been rendered with a somewhat hard grey pebbledash to unify the whole – a finish that has got even greyer with the passing years.

As the new wing had displaced the kitchen, at the edge of the farmyard a new detached building was created for this purpose, with a water pump and trough in front. Further developments soon took place in the yard, where a new hay barn and milking parlours were constructed abutting the existing farm buildings. So sensitively were all these additions carried out that they very soon merged imperceptibly with the older buildings.

Although Beatrix was able to stay at Hill Top for only about a month a year, she nevertheless set about furnishing the old house as her home. She brought up to Hill Top from London some of her family furniture and things given to her by Norman, and she became a familiar figure buying up old oak at farm sales round the district. Perhaps because she was an intermittent visitor, and as events turned out never lived full time in the house, her perception of Hill Top remained sharp and slightly dispassionate, and she was able to arrange and compose each room as a picture, her possessions positioned for dramatic effect. Now at last she could translate her ideas and feelings about spaces and places from imaginary interiors back into reality and she furnished Hill Top as she had said she would in her diary entries twenty-one years earlier.

BELOW *Sketch by Beatrix, c. 1905 (top), showing her ideas for her new wing on the left of the Hill Top farmhouse. The completed new wing (bottom) provided accommodation for the farm tenant, who vacated the old house for Beatrix's use. The elaborate iron gate, and a similar one at the entrance to the vegetable garden, were installed by Beatrix, as were the iron railings around her new drive.*

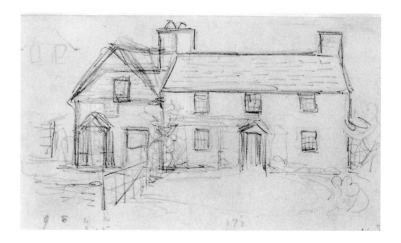

The first room to be sorted out was what she called the library, a room on the first floor of the new extension which became part of her domain: 'lighting the library fire, it was a great excitement. I laid the fire and lit it myself and it went straight up directly and gives great heat.' In the following year, 1907, she wrote that the firehouse – or hall as she called it – had been 'got straight ... I have got a pretty dresser and some old-fashioned chairs; and a warming pan that belonged to my great-grandmother; and Mr Warne's bellows which look well.' This was the beginning of the 'oak for the dining-room', which she added to over the years with a carved cupboard, a grandfather clock, a gate-leg table and farmhouse chairs.

Four years after she bought Hill Top, Beatrix purchased Castle Farm on the other side of Near Sawrey. She added the land to that of Hill Top, as the two farms conveniently ran together. In this, and other small purchases of land she had made in and around Near Sawrey, she had taken advice from a firm of local solicitors, W.H. Heelis and Son, who practised in Hawkshead and Ambleside. Beatrix dealt with one of two Heelis cousins, both called William, at the Hawkshead office which faces on to the square. The William who helped with Beatrix's transactions, the partner specializing in land transactions, had come from Appleby,

RIGHT *The former offices of W.H. Heelis and Son in Hawkshead, now the Beatrix Potter Gallery. William Heelis, who became Beatrix's husband, joined the firm as a partner in 1900 at the age of twenty-nine. The building dates from the seventeenth century and was re-fronted with its Venetian window in the early nineteenth century, possibly to the designs of a local architect, Ferdinando Taylor. On the right is Bend-or-Bump Cottage with its projecting slate-hung wing supported on massive vertical stone flags, similar to the ones on the porch at Hill Top.*

LEFT *A sketch of Bend-or-Bump Cottage and the bay window of the Heelis office from* The Tale of The Pie and The Patty-Pan. *Next to the door, a cat sits on a chest used to store the external shutters for the bay window. One shutter is shown propped against the wall. These shutters are still in use.*

the old county town of Westmorland, and was thus nicknamed by the locals 'Appleby Billie', to differentiate him from his cousin, 'Hawkshead Willie'. William attended farm auction sales on Beatrix's behalf and looked after her property while she was in London. Their friendship grew and developed and in 1913 they were married. Beatrix wrote to her cousin just before the marriage. 'He is 42 (I am 47) very quiet – dreadfully shy, but I'm sure he will be more comfortable married ... He is in every way satisfactory, well known in the district and respected.' And in another letter she added that it was 'the miserable feeling of loneliness that decided me at last'. William, who had spent much of his life in the area, shared Beatrix's growing love and enthusiasm for her adopted home and also understood her aspirations. He could help with her projects to buy land and improve her holdings. He also supported her aim to turn herself gradually into a respected Lake District farmer.

In October 1913, the month they were married, Beatrix published *The Tale of Pigling Bland*, based on sketches of pigs she had accumulated over many years. In it, Pig-wig, 'the perfectly lovely little black Berkshire pig', crosses a humped-back bridge hand in hand with Pigling Bland and dances 'over the hills and far away'. Perhaps this was an echo of William and Beatrix – although Beatrix somewhat humorously denied this: 'The portrait of two pigs arm in

RIGHT *Inside the former offices of W.H. Heelis and Son – now part of the Beatrix Potter Gallery. On the walls of William Heelis's office, above a mahogany bureau and the corner fireplace, hang two of a set of three black and white engravings entitled* The Rent Day, Reading the Will *and* Village Politicians. *They were engraved after paintings by D. Wilkie and were published between 1817 and 1825.*

LEFT *The pigeon-holes hang on the wall in the entrance room (above); upstairs is the clerk's desk, above which is part of the small library of law books the practice assembled (below).*

arm – looking at the sunrise is not a portrait of me and Mr Heelis, though it is where we used to walk on Sunday afternoons. When I want to put William into a book, it will have to be some very tall thin animal.'

The farmhouse at Castle Farm became the new home of Beatrix and William. She more than doubled it in size, extending the four-square late eighteenth-century house in length and adding a cross wing at one end with a drawing room on the first floor. On the front a pair of double doors sheltered by a pentice roof led into the garden, which sloped down to the road directly across from Hill Top's orchard. Castle Cottage – as Beatrix chose to call the farmhouse, although it was not a cottage in size but more a house in cottage style – was to be Beatrix's home for the rest of her life. But this did not mean Beatrix abandoned Hill Top; she continued to add to and nurture the house as a place to work and to entertain the increasing number of admirers who sought her out in the Lake District, many of whom were quite unaware that this was not her home. Hill Top was becoming inextricably tied up in her work as new stories were woven round it, but it was also becoming

ABOVE *Beatrix and William, photographed on the day of their engagement. They were married on 17 October 1913 in London in what the Westmorland Gazette described as 'the quietest of quiet manners'. According to members of the Heelis family, Beatrix and William returned from their marriage with a white bull calf in the back of the car.*

RIGHT AND FAR RIGHT *Castle Cottage, photographed by Rupert Potter on 13 July 1912, shortly after Beatrix bought it as part of Castle Farm, and as it is now much enlarged by Beatrix. The large first-floor window lights the upstairs drawing room.*

a work in its own right, a drawing made manifest, and part of the way Beatrix wished to project herself.

Gradually the Hill Top interior evolved into the wonderfully romantic place it is today. Beatrix translated her domestic feelings for spaces from paper to reality. The imaginary interiors in her books, in which the animals are cocooned in safe, cosy surroundings, became the richly furnished small spaces of Hill Top providing safety, security and a sense of belonging for its owner.

The parlour she furnished largely in mahogany with carved spoon-back chairs and a tripod table arranged in front of an elaborate marble fire surround. One of the bedrooms became a small sitting room where a glazed bookcase housed Peter Rabbit mementoes. In her bedroom, a carved oak four-poster bed was enclosed by

hangings she embroidered herself. Everywhere the furniture was overlain with personal treasures, valuable intrinsically or for their associations: Chinese and English porcelain; Staffordshire earthenware and Wedgwood jasper ware; oil paintings and tinsel pictures, ivories and horse brasses. The small room above the front door she actually called her treasure room. Densely arrayed with the smallest portable objects arranged in display cabinets, it was her cabinet of curiosities.

As we have seen, Beatrix keenly observed houses or parts of houses she visited and the memories of these spaces and the sketches she made of them came to influence strongly the way she laid out Hill Top. Her drawings of the oak hall at Gwaynynog came to life in the hall at Hill Top, where the door at the bottom of the stairs was widened to allow light

THIS PAGE AND OPPOSITE PAGE *A selection of the treasures with which Beatrix embellished her surroundings.*
From left to right: on the window ledge in the bedroom, two French dolls, which Beatrix said had belonged to her as a child —
although 'the shot silk dress is older'; china in the sitting-room cabinet, including a Wedgwood tea service decorated with scenes
from Beatrix's 'little books' and a dolls' tea set dating from about 1810; on the parlour mantelpiece beneath a Regency convex mirror,
a Mason-ware double-handled pottery mug and a pair of mid-nineteenth-century Staffordshire greyhounds with hares in their mouths;
the face of the grandfather clock in the hall, painted by James Wilson of Birmingham, c. 1892; mementoes and curios, such as bronze
figures of characters from the 'little books', beaded bags, miniature pots and a collection of snuff boxes, in the treasure room cabinet;
blue and white Staffordshire plates in a cupboard backing on to the old spiral staircase in the hall.

to flood down the eighteenth-century staircase into the hall and pick out carving on an oak cupboard, as at Gwaynynog. The green bed-hangings in her bedroom recall those of the room she stayed in at her grandmother's house, Camfield Place, while a chest of drawers surmounted by a mirror, in a corner of the upstairs sitting room, is precisely the combination she sketched at an old house in Winchelsea.

Beatrix's practice of taking inspiration from houses she knew and sketching places she remembered was very much in line with the thinking and practice of the day. She was creating Hill Top at a time when some of the leading thinkers — artists, architects and gardeners such as William Morris, Richard Norman Shaw and Gertude Jekyll — were seeking to re-define the essence of English arts and crafts and when there was also intense interest in the moral rightness of certain approaches to the decoration of interiors. Beatrix was right alongside them in the way she approached the furnishing of Hill Top, in the way she laid out her garden and indeed in buying up an old cottage in the first place. Her romantic interiors, too, fitted well the norms and prescriptions current at that time.

Before the 1830s such romantic interiors — where ancient or old objects are arranged in a picturesque way to create a certain atmosphere — were the exception rather than the rule. Until then rooms which were consciously designed were fitted out with matching new furniture to create a unified or harmonious look. In romantic interiors, on the other hand, the furniture and furnishings were an eclectic mixture of the old and the new, with pieces chosen for the way they could evoke times past.

The first romantic interiors were in grand houses put together by wealthy patrons; by the 1850s the fashion had spread to more modest houses and was being reflected by writers and artists, as in Nash's *Book of Mansions*, which showed rooms not necessarily as they were but as they might look if given a romantic patina. The appeal of recreating a microcosm of Old England extended beyond houses to the revival of medieval customs such as folk dancing and mumming plays — revivals to which incidentally Beatrix subscribed with enthusiasm.

Towards the end of the nineteenth century, romantic interiors had become so fashionable that various treatises and essays appeared on how to furnish a house in the romantic manner, and nearly all manuals on furnishing rooms contained instructions on how to create a romantic room. The influential architect Charles Eastlake explained: 'The smallest example of rare old porcelain, of ivory carving, of ancient metalwork, of enamels, of Venetian glass, of anything which illustrates good design and skilful workmanship should be acquired wherever possible, and treasured with the greatest care ... An Indian ginger-jar, a Flemish beer jug, a Japanese fan ... group them together as much as possible.' He was describing exactly the principles Beatrix had adopted at Hill Top.

The way Beatrix furnished Hill Top, with good examples of local oak furniture, also reflected how romantic interiors in the last quarter of the nineteenth century had moved away from using grand and important houses and contents as exemplars towards drawing inspiration from simple farmhouses and cottages and the rustic furniture they contained. William Morris was an influential pioneer of this change of approach, through his writings and many speeches as well as through the way he furnished his own house, Kelmscott Manor, near Oxford. Morris founded the Society for the Protection of Ancient Buildings, which stressed the value of studying traditional buildings and building techniques. He also strove to show how craftsmanship and the study of it was the key to good design. This new thinking had a social dimension too, propounded above all by John Ruskin, the well-known social reformer and art critic, who saw work by hand (as opposed to things made by machine) as being good both for those who produced the objects and for those who used them. Handmade objects, which revealed their origins and individuality of workmanship, were considered to be infinitely preferable to the perfection and standardization produced by machines.

In spearheading what became known as the Arts and Crafts movement, Morris and others saw straightforward, country furniture as epitomizing the pure, simple life, and village houses as seeming to have 'grown out of the soil and the lives that live on it'. Under the influence of this movement, romantic interiors became more localized, reflecting the cottage architecture of a region. Collectors began to seek out pieces of local furniture, and dealers in such things began to set up in business to satisfy demand. As early as the 1870s, the writer Harriet Martineau, who had settled in Ambleside, was bemoaning the fact that antiques dealers were scouring the Lake District for pieces of local carved oak furniture.

The Arts and Crafts movement was in many ways more than just a style: it was an ethos. It stressed the relationship or association between objects and life; objects could be important not just for their intrinsic worth but also for what they stood for or symbolized. In earlier times, serviceability of the products and scarcity of raw material resources from which they were constructed were dominant considerations. But under the new dispensation, simple country furniture came to be seen as evoking all that was noble in local craftsmen and craftsmanship and in their pure, rural way of life. And it was not just architects and

designers who were caught up in this thinking; artists and writers were too. Some of the more influential writers in the long term were American popular writers whose ideas found their way across the Atlantic between the 1880s and the First World War.

Old chairs, for instance, were seen no longer as mere supports for sitting; they had become reminders of an old morality, suffused with the spirit of those who had owned them. Old clocks could sum up all that was good about grandfathers, as expressed in the poem 'Grandfather's Clock' by the American Henry Clay Work:

It was bought on the morn of the day that he was born
And was always his treasure and pride
But it stopped short – never to go again –
When the old man died.

Writers also emphasized the significance of place: old objects could be put in 'new places' and gain new significance. Bedroom dressing tables and chests of drawers began to appear in sitting rooms (there is a chest in the upstairs sitting room at Hill Top with a dressing-table mirror on it) and, most popular of all, grandfather clocks began to migrate from living rooms to stairs. So significant did this trend become that another American poet, H.W. Longfellow, wrote a poem 'The Old Clock on the Stairs':

Half way up the stairs it stands
And points and beckons with its hands.

Beatrix installed a clock on the stairs at Hill Top, on the half-landing, which she immortalized in *The Tale of Samuel Whiskers*.

Longfellow painted another vivid domestic image in his ballad 'The Courtship of Miles Standish', this time of a spinning wheel in the parlour. (By now the name parlour was associated with a small sitting room rather than the best bedroom. Most spinning had also become mechanized and was carried out in factories.)

So shall it be with your own, when the spinning wheel shall no longer
Hum in the house of the farmer, and fill its chambers with music
Then shall the mothers, reproving, relate how it was in their childhood
Praising the good old times, and the days of Priscilla the spinner!

This widely read poem reflected, or possibly influenced, a revival of interest in hand-spinning wheels and particularly in their placement by the hearth as decoration. Beatrix followed this fashion: she acquired three. Two flank the fire in the hall at Hill Top, while the third, a much more elaborate and delicate mahogany one, is next to the fire in the parlour.

OPPOSITE *Beatrix sketched this view of a bedroom inside Derwent Cottage, Winchelsea, when she stayed there in February 1900. It was a view that must have stayed in her mind, for, when she came to furnish Hill Top, the image of a mirror on a chest of drawers next to a small sash-window was one she re-created there.*

RIGHT *Sketch of a spinning wheel by Beatrix intended as the endpage for an illustrated booklet of the nursery rhyme 'Three Little Mice Sat Down to Spin', c. 1892, which was never published.*

ABOVE *Photograph by Rupert Potter (left) of the hall at Hill Top, showing the cast-iron range in the house when Beatrix bought it, and a photograph also by Rupert Potter (right) showing the fireplace after the range had been replaced by a hearth-fire and crane (dates for the photographs are unknown).*

RIGHT *The hall today at Hill Top with a range reinstated. On the left is the American rocking chair from Belmount, Rebecca Owen's house on the outskirts of Hawkshead.*

OPPOSITE *Watercolour by Beatrix of the kitchen fire at Spout House, Far Sawrey, c. 1910, showing the kettle hanging from the fire-crane on a 'reckon' or strap-hanger. The range was used as the background for the kitchen scenes in The Tale of Pigling Bland.*

Equally influential, it seems, were a few simple lines Longfellow wrote in 'The Hanging of the Crane' about a ceremony in a new house:

O fortunate, O happy day
When a new household finds its place ...
So said the guests in speech and song
As in the chimney, burning bright
We hung the iron crane tonight,
And merry was the feast and long.

Because of their association with wood or peat fires, fire-cranes for supporting cooking pots over the fire were another reminder of pre-industrial days and therefore came to be seen as pure and untainted, unlike coal, which epitomized all things dirty and industrial. It became fashionable to take out coal grates, open up the old wide chimney recesses and install fire-cranes. Later in life Beatrix removed the iron range in the hall at Hill Top – also immortalized in *The Tale of Samuel Whiskers* – and put in a crane within a whitewashed recess. Unfortunately the arrangements were entirely impractical, as the fire would not draw properly, and, in response to the popularity of her stories and the expectations of the many visitors who come to Hill Top, an old range has now been put back.

The growing interest in cottages and their furnishings coincided with a rapid increase in the number of tourists visiting the countryside from the ever-swelling industrial cities. This was particularly true of the Lake District which was within reach of the huge industrial conurbations of Liverpool, Manchester, Leeds and Bradford. Visitors were able to see at first

hand what the Arts and Crafts writers were talking about, to see in country life ideals lost in the towns.

For many the interest led to a desire to buy up old cottages and farmhouses as well as their furniture. Beatrix's choice of Hill Top was paralleled by others. John Ruskin, for

instance, had bought a small, old farmhouse, Brantwood, above Coniston Water in 1871. It didn't stay small for long as he greatly extended it, but he chose to adapt an old house for his own needs rather than build anew. He recognized in the farmhouse an image of what he called 'organic, natural rightness, and wholeness with its surroundings, without the burden of taste or conscious architecture'. He was buying a building that seemed rooted in the landscape and in so doing was buying himself roots. In the south of England, the actress Ellen Terry bought Smallhythe, an old farmhouse in Kent, and fitted it out with oak, pewter, copper and hand-made rugs; and writer Rudyard Kipling settled in Batemans, a seventeenth-century house built for a Wealden iron master in Sussex.

It was not just outsiders moving into the countryside who chose to distil the essence of country living through choosing fine examples of vernacular, or local, buildings and fitting them out with romantic interiors accentuating local crafts. Some local families too altered their houses to highlight their lineage and emphasize distinctiveness by re-displaying their rooms with an antiquarian overlay.

The Browne family had lived at Townend Farm, Troutbeck, since at least the early seventeenth century. In the 1890s, George Browne set about adding to the impressive stock of oak furniture in his house by carving new pieces with retrospective dates and by 'improving' the earlier pieces with extra carving. Much of what visitors now see (the house is open to the public), including the grandfather clock at the top of the stairs, bears the hallmark of this last Browne. Beatrix was one of those who did not approve of everything George Browne did: 'the footboards of the splendid old bedstead have been covered with copied old patterns by the tiresome Mr Browne. Likewise the cradle …' Ironically it is now at times difficult to differentiate all of George Browne's work from that of his predecessors.

All this highlights interesting differences of perception. Both Beatrix and Ruskin thought it quite proper to enlarge

and almost rebuild old houses, using local craftsmen and taking inspiration from local forms of building – Beatrix at Hill Top and Castle Cottage, and Ruskin at Brantwood. But Beatrix was against improving old furniture with copies or interpretations of old patterns, however good the craftsmanship, however local the craftsman.

Perhaps Beatrix was more in favour of George Browne's new pieces. She certainly seems to have been in sympathy with many exponents of the Arts and Crafts movement who were keen that crafts should be revived to create local employment. Adapting or enlarging houses or building anew were seen as ways of achieving this. As well as her new farm buildings, she was to have the opportunity to adapt several buildings and also later to design and build, in the local style, a completely new house.

Around the Lake District there are other examples of this Arts and Crafts approach. Several cottages, built in the period 1900–20 of local materials, reflect vernacular traditions extremely well. Many had romantic interiors, with carefully arranged pieces of good old oak and mahogany, spiced with treasured pieces of metalwork, glass or ceramics. Houses built by the local architect Dan Gibson, such as Birkett Houses in the Lythe valley and Keldwyth in Windermere, typify this approach, as do the houses along the east side of Windermere designed by the architect C.F.A. Voysey. Unfortunately in most of them the movable furniture, and sometimes even the panelling and other fixtures, has been dispersed. So Hill Top is today even more significant than when Beatrix first conceived it.

Looking out through the small-paned sash-window in the hall at Hill Top. The sashes are glazed with crown glass which slightly distorts the light, creating watery patterns on the walls and floor. In a letter to Louie Warne (Harold Warne's daughter) Beatrix made small sketches of the way the crooked panes of glass in her bedroom window distorted the sheep she could see outside, giving them a zigzag appearance.

A TOUR OF HILL TOP

LEFT *The substantial oak front door at Hill Top is unusual in having nine raised and fielded panels. It is hung on long iron strap-hinges. The classical, cast-iron door knocker was almost certainly added by Beatrix.*

RIGHT *Beatrix, photographed by an American visitor, outside the porch at Hill Top in the summer of 1913. She is wearing the suit of grey wool, from local Herdwick sheep, that she had on for her wedding day and was to wear for the next twenty years or so. Being conscious of her thin hair — the result of illness when she was younger — she nearly always covered her head with some sort of hat.*

HILL TOP FARMHOUSE is now a shrine to Beatrix Potter: its rooms are preserved almost as she left them. It is a shrine she set up for herself. In the six small rooms — hall, parlour, bedroom, treasure room, sitting room and 'new' room — she arranged her possessions with care and precision and kept them as a place for work and for entertaining. She added to and rearranged the furniture over the years while she lived across the road at Castle Cottage on the other side of Near Sawrey. After her death a few of her belongings from Castle Cottage were moved to Hill Top in accordance with her wishes in order that this, her final work, should be preserved.

Hill Top with Esthwaite Water beyond and, in the distance, Wetherlam and the Langdale Pikes. Approached from Near Sawrey, Hill Top hardly seems to be at the top of a hill; but viewed from the south end of Esthwaite Water, the land in front of the farm buildings is seen to drop sharply towards the lake.

LEFT *William Heelis sitting in the porch at Hill Top on one of the chairs which came from his office (photographer and date unknown).*

RIGHT *Ribby, based on one of the Sawrey cats, arriving to borrow yeast in* The Tale of Samuel Whiskers. *The setting is clearly based on the front door at Hill Top.*

OPPOSITE *Looking across the hall or firehouse towards the stairs at Hill Top. On the ceiling the line of the partition, which Beatrix removed, can be seen.*

The Hall or Firehouse

The front door faces south and is sheltered by a simple porch, formed from four large slabs of local stone, two vertical pieces for the sides and two more forming a small ridge roof supported on timber brackets projecting from the wall. Beatrix added a row of wooden coat hooks just under one of the timber bearers on the sheltered south-west side of the porch.

The stones for the porch came from an outcrop of rock near Outgate, just north of Hawkshead, which was quarried for the immensely large and comparatively thin sheets of stone the geology allowed. These stones are quite a feature of buildings in the Hawkshead area. They were used not only for porches but also as walls of buildings, such as in Bend-or-Bump Cottage, next to the Heelis office in Hawkshead village, where the jettied upper storey is carried on walls formed from vertical stones.

On a sunny day the porch at Hill Top is warm and inviting. A photograph Beatrix took a few years before she bought Hill Top shows Mrs Beckett, the wife of the Potters' coach-man who always stayed at Hill Top, her son and Mrs Preston, wife of the then tenant, all standing just by the porch. Beatrix herself was photographed leaning against one side by an American visitor in 1913. One of the few photos of William Heelis shows him seated just within its shade.

The front door beyond the porch is substantial, of oak and in nine raised fielded panels with a door knocker almost certainly put on by Beatrix. The door opens directly into the old farm firehouse, what Beatrix called the hall. Once visitors have adjusted to the comparative gloom of the interior, the first view of the firehouse with its glossy oak furniture, polished range and shafts of light filtering through the old glass of its small-paned window is one that they always remember.

When Beatrix bought Hill Top the firehouse had been partitioned to create a narrow hall running towards the stairs that gave privacy to the main room of the house. It was an alteration found in many houses in the area as the use of spaces changed in response to increasing formality. Beatrix undid this alteration, reinstating the large central firehouse space but leaving tell-tale marks in the ceiling of the groove which held the vertical timbers of the partition wall.

Until coal was transported into the area towards the end of the eighteenth century, peat and wood were the staple fuels. The Hill Top firehouse would have been heated by a large open-hearth fire against the gable wall, sheltered within a recess almost spanning the width of the room and lit by a small window in the front wall. The smoke was gathered into a large stone hood supported at ceiling level on a fire-beam which is still visible above the iron range. In order to burn coal, stronger draughts had to be provided through smaller narrower flues, and by raising the fire off the ground. When coal arrived at Hill Top, a new flue was built within the old chimney recess. This fed into the chimney hood and an iron grate was installed, later supplanted by an iron range with ovens and a hot water boiler. The space to its left was turned into a roomy cupboard blocking the fire window — still visible within as a recess. To the right of the chimney are two further cupboards, one of which backs on to spiral stairs which used to give access to the first floor.

The present range is an almost identical copy of one in the house when Beatrix bought Hill Top. It was installed in the early 1980s and replaced the fire-crane and iron basket grate which Beatrix put in when she took out the range in the 1920s.

ABOVE *The hall and its furnishings are immortalized in* The Tale of Samuel Whiskers. *Here Tom Kitten is ready to spring up the chimney into the cavernous space above the range, a remnant of the large chimney hood which once drew up smoke from the open hearth fire.*

OPPOSITE *Around the table in the hall are turned chairs with rush seats, probably from a furniture maker in Eskdale. The paper covering the walls and ceiling was originally put on by Beatrix in 1906; the present paper is a screen-printed copy made in 1987.*

Hanging to one side of the fire surround is the warming pan that belonged to Beatrix's great-grandmother and which is unusual in that it was designed to hold hot water rather than coals. On the other side are the bellows that came from Norman Warne, and her clogs and hat. And framing the fireplace are two spinning wheels by the hearth, symbols of domestic simplicity and harmony.

Until potatoes and wheat became available generally, the staple food cooked on the open-hearth fires of the Lake District was unleavened oat cake, known as clapbread. Clapbread is made from a mixture of fine oatmeal and water, kneaded until smooth and then clapped out to form a thin round bread which was cooked on a back-stone, or metal griddle, over the open fire. Such unleavened bread would keep for several weeks if stored in oak cupboards in the firehouse. Such oak cupboards, of two storeys and often embellished with carvings, are the glory of Lake District farmhouses. They were usually, but not always, built into the partition which separated the firehouse from the parlour and were often decorated with fine incised motifs incorporating the initials of their owners along with the date they were made or installed. In all Beatrix came to own a dozen such cupboards, one at Hill Top and the rest in farmhouses she bought later.

THE FIREHOUSE

In Hill Top the built-in cupboard did not survive; in its place Beatrix installed one with a date of 1667 bought at a farm auction at 'a little out of the way farm near Crook, a forlorn dirty little place, everyone dead except an old man removed to an infirmary'. She said it was her 'favourite cupboard. It is very plain, except the middle, fixed panel, which has good carving . . . The cupboard . . . was detached when I bought it . . . But like all others now detached it had originally been a fixture. It is unusually long in shape. The 4 doors fasten with thumb pieces, and the doors are hung on pins — i.e. iron rods instead of hinges.' The

cupboard was in 'a dark little kitchen . . . amongst broken debris and lumber . . . it had belonged to the aged wife, the neighbours said she had refused good offers in her lifetime for the "sideboard"'. Like most sale-goers, Beatrix expected to get a bargain but on this occasion the price was pushed up by two other knowledgeable people, an unknown lady and gentleman, as well as a second auctioneer and she had to pay £21 10s, a considerable sum then for a cupboard which in fact is far from perfect (having at some time lost its base, which was why Beatrix thought it such an odd shape).

The carvings on these cupboards include many motifs. Several are peculiar to the Lake District and their disposition varies across the valleys. Beatrix wrote with knowledge about all this to her American correspondents: 'I have a theory (only my own) that the craftsmen who carved our designs were imitating the runic interlacing. It would be too much to say that their patterns were developed from Scandinavia . . . but I do think some one of the old joiners and carvers must have been familiar with such patterns as those on the Gosforth Cross [an early tenth-century tall, carved, stone cross with wonderful interlaced patterns].'

The chairs in the hall are an interesting mixture of farmhouse furniture, somewhat grander dining chairs and a few pieces of American furniture. The simple turned chairs

LEFT *Beatrix was distressed to see local, carved oak-press cupboards, such as this one, 'riven out of ancestral cottages'. Above her cupboard, bought at a farm sale, hang eight plates painted with animals and birds by her father, Rupert.*

RIGHT *On 11 October 1940, Beatrix sent her thoughts on pieces of her oak furniture to Bertha Mahoney of the Boston Bookshop. This page is part of a draft of the letter, dated the same day.*

1667

My favourite court cupboard. An
unusual long shape - the centre panel is
very fine. The doors are fastened with
wooden thumb bits, and they swing & hang
on iron pins, instead of hinges. The centre
panel is fixed. This panel & the barge board
are the only portions
which
are
carved.

5 Sets

5 half rondels   5

half 4 + 4 + 4 half
rondels

A very beautiful chest, rich colour & good carving
but not local. I bought it from an old woman
who lived in Thimble Hall; but she said her mother
came from Nantwich in Cheshire or Shropshire.
The lock is old but not original lock.
It is more carved upon than any local
piece.

with rush seats arranged round the centre table are nice examples of 'thrown' chairs – 'our common (by no means despicable) rush bottomed cottage chair', as Beatrix described them, which in many farmhouses formed the basic seating along with benches and stools. Those at Hill Top could be Eskdale chairs as they show all the hallmarks of a turner called Brockleback, whose chair workshop near the entrance to the church in Eskdale Green, in the west of the Lake District, flourished until the early years of the twentieth century.

Around the edge of the hall are a pair of Chippendale-style mahogany chairs which Beatrix said came from 'a garret over my husband's office ... rather elaborately carved Chippendale' and a 'Queen Anne style fiddle-back chair which had been painted green in a farmhouse in Wales'. Next to the fire the rocking chair is part of the American furniture she bought from Rebecca Owen, who lived at Belmount on the outskirts of Hawkshead. ('Rebecca Owen ... is an American who has lived for a great many years near Hawkshead – a remarkable old person, must be nearly 80; lipstick, pink nails, a handsome car, and lives in a large house *alone*.') The spindles in the rocking chair 'go through above the back rest and are finished with knobs. The rocking chair is a particularly nice one to sit in!' The rocking chair must have been one of the last pieces to have been put into the hall – it was still at Belmount when Beatrix was writing about it in 1940 just before Rebecca Owen died.

ABOVE *Anna Maria, in* The Tale of Samuel Whiskers, *running across the hall towards the bread-crock, full of rising dough, which has been covered with a cloth and set to warm by the hearth.*

OPPOSITE *The dresser and long-case clock in the hall. Oil lamps and candles were a feature of Hill Top because Beatrix refused to connect electricity to the house.*

The hall was the second room Beatrix 'got straight', after the library. As well as the old-fashioned chairs she mentioned, one of her first purchases was a 'pretty dresser with crooked legs' in pale oak, decorated with mahogany banding and inlaid with shell medallions on the doors . It is not known where she bought this but it must have been almost new when it arrived at Hill Top. It now displays a collection of blue and white ware, some Chinese – the five plates with scalloped edges on the lower shelf painted with flowers and butterflies and dating from around 1800 – and some Staffordshire earthenware, blue willow pattern and two portrait bowls, one of Lord Nelson and the other of George III and Queen Charlotte.

Next to the dresser, facing the front door and in a recess adjoining the doors to the stairs, is a tall oak long-case clock. This was made by Thomas Barrow of Stockport in around 1785 and has a pretty dial painted by James Wilson of Birmingham. The very same clock appears in the drawings Beatrix made for *The Tailor of Gloucester*, her second book, published in 1902 long before she bought Hill Top. The interiors for this story were based on sketches she did in and around cottages in the Cotswolds and also at Melford Hall in Suffolk, the home of her cousin, Ethel, Lady Hyde Parker. Perhaps that is where the clock came from.

The furniture forms the bones of the hall. As elsewhere in the house, it is accompanied by 'treasures' collected by Beatrix over the years she owned Hill Top,

arranged for picturesque effect. The space on the mantelshelf is shared by some Doulton stoneware jugs, an eighteenth-century Staffordshire bust of John Wesley and two wooden, jointed Peter Rabbit toys. Above the oak cupboard hang a set of plates decorated with animals and birds by Beatrix's father Rupert. Below these on the cupboard top are arranged a Chinese jug, a late eighteenth-century Liverpool creamware bowl, a ginger jar and a cast bronze of a leaping frog, rather curiously wearing sandals.

To the right of the window are two small paintings, one of Swiss cattle by Randolph Caldecott and the other of Holy Island by Lord Leighton, both from her father's collection. Beatrix said that she had 'the greatest admiration' for Caldecott's illustrations, 'a jealous appreciation' as she further called it, but she seems to have had less respect for his oils. The Swiss cattle picture she wrote was 'painted on a bit of paste board, with a small brush. The cows are very good, but the general effect is wanting in light – as though it had been painted on brown paper and sunk in. On the back of the cow's picture is an unfinished view of Caldecott's house . . .'

Hanging on the ceiling beam are an eel spear and a percussion cap shotgun – perhaps bought from farm sales. The long-handled three-pronged spear would have been used for catching eels in the dykes on the low-lying land in the south of the Lake District.

The all-enclosing warm feel of the hall has much to do with the tightly patterned wallpaper, green and white, which runs all over the ceiling as well as the walls. This was originally put on by Beatrix soon after she bought the house, and in putting it over the ceiling she was copying cottage fashion. The paper was replaced in 1987 with a screen-printed copy as the original had been painted over.

In front of the fire is a peg rug, a hard-wearing rug made from scraps of waste fabric hooked, or threaded, on to a sack-cloth backing. Such rugs, sometimes called hookey rugs, were widely made in winter evenings all over the north of England. Over part of the remainder of the floor, a sea-grass mat with a pink border covers the stone flags of local blue Brathay stone, worn smooth by generations of clog-shod feet.

ABOVE *Beatrix was involved in creating the two Peter Rabbit toys on the mantelpiece only a few years after* The Tale of Peter Rabbit *was first published. A few years later, during the election campaign of 1910, she became actively involved in fighting against free trade, to protect the south London toy trade.*

RIGHT *A corner of the hall with the window to the right of the front door.*

The Parlour

Opening off the hall, the parlour was once the main bedroom. Like the hall it has a window to the front of the house, but it is less deep, sharing the depth of the house with what is now a small narrow cupboard. Double doors open out of the parlour into part of this cupboard, which may once have housed the parlour bed. Such bed-cupboards are not common in the Lake District – they are found more frequently in parts of Yorkshire – but they are not unknown. One, complete with its bed, survived until recently at Waitby, near Kirkby Stephen. The doors would have closed off the bed in the daytime from the rest of the room.

What the parlour looked like when Beatrix bought Hill Top we do not know, but almost certainly it did not have the grandeur it now exhibits, resulting from the over-sized, and imposing, marble chimneypiece she installed. She also panelled the walls in pine-boarding, decorated above the fireplace with flat pilasters.

The room is set out as a small drawing room, the rich mahogany furnishings of which contrast strongly with the oak country furniture in the hall. This reflects what Beatrix said she would like to do in the diary she wrote in Oxford all those years before: 'Chippendale in the drawing room' and oak in the dining room. The drawing-room furniture is not quite Chippendale, but it is mostly mahogany (as Chippendale nearly always is). The ensemble includes many of the elements found in larger rooms: French-style occasional chairs upholstered with carved mahogany frames arranged around a small tripod table with a vase baluster, a prie-dieu (prayer chair), and a fold-over card table with claw and ball feet. There is also a rosewood work table.

BELOW *Looking through the parlour window at the knarled stem of the climbing wisteria. On the left of the window ledge is a miniature horizontal sundial made by G. Davies of Leeds in 1900.*

OPPOSITE *Around the mahogany tripod table are part of a set of four French-style, spoonback upholstered chairs. In the background is a prie-dieu or prayer chair, so called for its tall back and low seat which could be used to kneel on.*

LEFT *A pair of double doors in the corner of the parlour enclose what was possibly the bed-cupboard, a small square room, papered with the same paper as the hall, and just long enough to take a bed. In front of the doors is a mahogany flap-top, nineteenth-century card table, on which is a rosewood writing box inlaid with mother of pearl.*

RIGHT *The marble, Adam-style fireplace put in by Beatrix dominates the small parlour. The pine boarding on two of the walls was also added by her and matches the colour of the earlier bed and cupboard doors opposite the window. On either side of the fireplace hang silhouettes, three of which came from Belmount.*

Overlaying all this are 'treasures', which give the room its richness. These are a mixture of the precious and the popular. In the corner cupboard (which has been given a glazed door) there is Chinese and English porcelain as well as an Edward VII coronation tea pot with lid surmounted by a crown (an item which appears in *The Tale of The Pie and The Patty-Pan*). On the mantelpiece we find Staffordshire figurines of greyhounds and an early Mason-ware double-handled mug. There are a pair of Punch and Judy cast-iron door stops on the hob grate, and an Italian red lacquer box, inset with wax impressions of classical gem-stones, on the work-table. Near the door stands a small, oriental cabinet decorated with geometrical parquetry work and ornate copper mounts. The fireplace is flanked by small framed silhouettes.

Some of the silhouettes came from Belmount. Coincidentally, in sorting out Rebecca Owen's papers after her death, Beatrix came across a pedigree of her mother's family traced back to 'Simon Sackett 1602–45, colonist, ... understood to have been a native of Ely'. She wrote of three of the silhouettes: 'I think these are Miss Owen's maternal grandparents and Aunt Sackett.' The 'shades', as Beatrix called them, are oval in simple cushion frames. One shows a lady in a bonnet.

Like her furniture, many of the treasures came from auction sales, often from farms. She went on collecting right up to 1940, when she bought several pieces at a sale at Coniston including 'a Bristol punch bowl, early 18th century ... it has written in the bottom, "Fill every man his glass". 4/6 with 7 assorted articles, some useful. It has been repaired but it gives me pleasure; decorated in the Chinese style, in cobalt and manganese.'

ABOVE *An unpublished drawing of Duchess and Ribby for* The Tale of The Pie and The Patty-Pan, *1902, showing, on the table, Beatrix's coronation tea pot which is now in the parlour cupboard. The interior was based on Mrs Lord's cottage at Lakefield in Sawrey.*

BELOW *A framed drawing of the Potter coat of arms hangs to the left of the parlour window.*

To the left of the window hang the Potter coat of arms (on the right Potter quartering Moore, on the left Crompton). It was through the Cromptons, her paternal grandmother's family, that Beatrix was associated with the Lake District; her great-grandfather had a farm at Holme Ground, near Coniston, which she was to buy back. Around the rest of the walls are a small collection of paintings, some perhaps coming from the homes of family members. There are landscapes by Charlotte Nasmyth, John Brett, W.L. Turner and W.R. Buckley, depicting scenes in Scotland, Yorkshire and the Lake District. There is also a small oil painting by Randolph Caldecott, 'a hunting piece; good, but rather flat and finicky as a painting ... he painted a small number of oils, tentatively ...' Beatrix seems to have kept two Caldecott oils after her mother's death (the other one is in the hall). Curiously she sent the watercolours, which she admired more than the oils, to a Manchester art gallery.

A small, oval needlework picture of a woman in mourning hanging near the window is one of the few pieces in the house to have connections with the Heelis family. It is inscribed in memory of Emma Corbett and has a label on the back saying it had come from 'Mrs Heelis, Esthwaite Mount. Bought at Mr W D Heelis' sale. June 7.34.' (This Mrs Heelis was the widow of W.D. Heelis, 'Hawkshead Willie', William's partner, Esthwaite Mount, Colthouse, had been their home.)

After Beatrix's death a small part of her book collection was brought from Castle Cottage to Hill Top where it is housed in the tall wall cupboard behind the door. The rest went to her husband's family.

LEFT *Treasures in the glazed mahogany corner cupboard in the parlour include an Edward VII coronation tea pot, with a pink crown lid, above it a large Derby tea pot and matching plate, c. 1810–1820, and, on the lowest shelf, a Kangxi porcelain saucer dish, c. 1710, behind a pair of Qianlong porcelain figures, c. 1750. The three silhouettes hanging to one side were, according to notes on the back, bought by Beatrix in Aspatria, west Cumbria.*

Stairs

The staircase wing was added to the rear of Hill Top in the late eighteenth century. Supplementing the small, tight, oak spiral staircase that had led up from within the firehouse, the new staircase is an elegant and rather grand, dog-leg affair, with slim turned balusters and a curved handrail. It is not unusual for Lake District farmhouses to have well-detailed stairs, and several houses around Near Sawrey and Hawkshead have examples similar to the one at Hill Top.

The stairs are lit halfway up by a comparatively large mullion and transom window with leaded light glazing. The glazing is protected by a turned baluster rail, behind which is a small-scale alabaster copy of *The Reading Girl* by the early nineteenth-century Italian sculptor Pietro Magni. The statue sits on a plain, seventeenth-century joined stool bought in 1940 from Mr Ellwood's sale at Torver. 'The old man's father had been a clergyman and collected oak, in fact, several pieces were suspect of having been cleared out of Torver Church in the last century ...' Beatrix called it a 'coffin' stool – 'I wonder if our name "coffin stool" is merely local? Its explanation is an old custom of resting the coffin on two stools in order to be safe from rats!'

On the half-landing is the grandfather clock seen with Tabitha Twitchit on the stairs in *The Tale of Samuel Whiskers*. Made by Schofields, a Rochdale firm, it is inlaid with walnut. With its tall hooded top adorned with brass orbs, it looks very similar to the one Beatrix painted at her Uncle Fred's house at Gwaynynog.

On one of the staircase walls, and rather squeezed into the space, is a large canvas by the Genoese painter Giovanni Castiglione, entitled *Thanksgiving After The Flood*. Opposite it is a copy of *The Hon Mrs Graham* by Gainsborough – one of a large number of copies made of this popular portrait.

LEFT *Looking down the stairs to the half-landing with its tall oak mullion and transom window, which was put in in the eighteenth century, when the staircase wing was added. On the right hangs the painting,* Thanksgiving After The Flood, *by Giovanni Castiglione.*

RIGHT *The grandfather clock on the stairs, from* The Tale of Samuel Whiskers. *Tabitha Twitchit is looking for her son.*

At the time the new staircase was put in, a landing was made on the first floor. This provides a space off which the rooms now open. Before that, the oak spiral stairs would have led straight into a large room over the firehouse, which in turn would have led into a second, smaller room. When the best bedroom was still downstairs in the parlour, the rooms on the first floor would have been used for sleeping – by children and members of the household not housed downstairs – or for the storage of oats (the staple diet), barley (for malting beer) and fruit (from the orchards). When the first-floor rooms were given over exclusively to sleeping, a granary was created away from the house adjoining the farm buildings.

There are now three rooms at the front of the house, as the larger of the original two was subdivided. The room over part of the firehouse Beatrix used as her own bedroom. The two others at the front are what became a small sitting room and the one she called her 'treasure room'. At the rear, a further room was created in the new wing added by Beatrix. This is now called the 'new room' and it was here she drew and wrote.

On the landing, in front of the bedroom doors, is a low blanket chest of oak, carved with lunettes along the rail and lozenges in the two panels. Beatrix called this 'a fine old chest from Shropshire ... more carved upon than any local piece'. She contrasted the rich red of its colour, 'almost as warm as mahogany', with the light, golden grey of much Westmorland oak furniture. She believed the red hue could have been the result of treatment with madder, a red vegetable dye. Sitting on the chest are a Staffordshire jug and two-handled tureen stand.

OPPOSITE *On the landing stands a carved oak blanket chest Beatrix bought from an old lady who lived in Thimble Hall, a small jettied town house in the centre of Hawkshead which Beatrix later came to own. Above the chest hangs a watercolour* Two Girls on a Jetty *painted in 1884 by George Dunlop Leslie.*

BELOW *Samuel Whiskers pushing the rolling pin across the landing in* The Tale of Samuel Whiskers. *The turkey stair runner and rug shown on the floor no longer exist.*

Bedroom

Beatrix only ever used this room occasionally between the time she bought the farm and her marriage to William. But this did not stop her adding to and re-arranging the furniture and making alterations until it matched her aspirations. The room as it is seen today was not finally completed until around 1940, some thirty-five years after she bought the house.

The fine example of a seventeenth-century Lake District tester bed was bought by Beatrix from a farm near Warcop, not far from Appleby. The tester, or ceiling to the bed, has sixteen panels, each carved with lozenge design. The headboard has an upper tier of panels decorated with a stylized flower pattern under arcading, a pattern which Beatrix noted was similar to a piece she had been shown years before in an old fortified house at Darnick, near Melrose, Scotland, whose owners had said the piece was 'by tradition *English*, and acquired in a raid. A cupboard seems a curious and cumbrous article to steal but undoubtedly the carving was of the same design as that of my 4 post bed!'

Beatrix started embroidering the green cotton damask hangings in 1935, writing: 'I have been embroidering a valance for an old 4 post bed. I used some old green damask and worked on it with old gold coloured silk.' She was still working on the valance when in hospital in 1939. She finished off the curtains while recuperating, 'I dare say finishing the curtains will be nice amusement if I cannot go out much.'

ABOVE *A patchwork quilt covers the horsehair and feather mattresses on the bed.*

OPPOSITE *Next to the tester bed, bought by Beatrix at a farm near Appleby, stands the American Windsor chair from Belmount. Above it is a framed print of* The Madonna and Child *which has been highlighted with gold paint and coloured with pencils. The rope mattress supports of the bed can be seen threaded through the front rail of the frame.*

Given that the colour of the bed curtains echoes the green curtains around her childhood bed at Camfield Place, perhaps they are indeed the same curtains as, after her grandmother's death, the bed became hers. The mattress is supported on a network of rope threaded through holes in the frame. Writing at the height of the Second World War to American friends and musing about the possibility of an invasion, she felt that the one thing that could not be saved was the 'wonderful old bedstead too heavy to move in a hurry'.

Next to the bed stands a small, slight Windsor chair, stained a dark greeny-grey colour. It is one of the pieces Beatrix acquired from Rebecca Owen of Belmount, and is of great interest because it is of American origin. Many of Rebecca Owen's belongings, which it seems had been brought from the United States around 1900, were sold in London after her death, but Beatrix was able to buy a few things at a smaller sale in Windermere. Her possession of these few American pieces fuelled a lively discussion with Bertha Mahoney of the Boston Bookshop on the subject of the differences between English and American furniture. Beatrix seems to have spent much time leafing through a copy of a book on colonial furniture by Lockwood, sent by Bertha Mahoney — 'I could go through these volumes forever' — and this prompted her to write about the Windsor chair from Belmount, saying Miss Owen had told her that it had been made by the Shakers about 1800.

roundels, slightly cusped
are the principal motif in
the carving on back of my
four post bedstead.

tulips & pomegranate
repeated, left & right

← arched panel in centre

← barge board

grapes & leaf —

this "running" pattern occurs

on pieces made at Ulverston — I consider the patterns
on this chest are an old design, but the chest itself is not very
ancient; abt 1700. It is interesting because it belonged to
the Fells, an Ulverston family, iron masters. It is unlucky
that the iron strap hinges are missing. It is a large
chest with a drawer.   Many of the carvings in Mr L's book
are familiar. But he shows very few of our most frequent
foundation patterns — the ∞ and the ↄ — I notice that
where he draws the ∞ it is inverted; the ↄ is
printed. I take notice of this because

OPPOSITE *Another page of the draft letter to Bertha Mahoney (see page 53). Beatrix writes about decoration on her bedroom chest and also comments on illustrations of carved American furniture in Mr Lockwood's book, '. . . he shows very few of our most frequent foundation patterns', such as the figure of eight or the S shape.*

LEFT *Above the heavily carved blanket chest in the bedroom hangs what Beatrix called a 'curious picture' of birds. It is in the Chinese style and was probably painted by Samuel Dixon in the 1750s.*

BELOW *On the chest is a carved oak box with a sloping top which houses Beatrix's bible. It is of a type often appropriately called a bible-box.*

Just inside the door is an oak blanket chest Beatrix believed had once belonged to the Fells, a well-known Ulverston family of iron workers. She did not say how she acquired it. The chest has a top lid, three carved panels and a running decoration along the top rail. She thought it 'a good example of copying. I do not think it is earlier than 1700, but the patterns were 16th, early 17th, the round Norman arch — the pomegranate, and the roundels, and the tulip or fleur-de-lys. The pomegranate is traditionally the symbol of Catherine of Aragon, but I have never met with the Tudor rose, which is rather strange as High Furness is so near Lancaster. This Ulverston chest has a running vine leaf, a leaf-and-bunch-of-grapes design which occurs on Ulverston cupboards. I should be inclined to derive this pattern from the influence of Furness Abbey. I think it occurs on tiles.'

Flanking the chest are a pair of tall, cane-seated chairs, probably dating from the 1700s which were bought 'from a tradesman's humble sale'. Beatrix noted how 'both of the backs are frankly repaired. I fancy these very tall-backed Charles II chairs had a failing of getting tipped backwards.'

The carved English oak and the simple chairs contrast strongly with three pieces of Chinese-influenced lacquer-work. There is an eighteenth-century Oriental cabinet made up from decorated lacquer panels, a cabinet on a stand painted in imitation of Oriental lacquer-work, and a gold and lacquer mirror over the fireplace. Above the oak chest hang three eighteenth-century gouache pictures of birds, all in one frame; they look Chinese but are now thought to

have been painted by Samuel Dixon. On the back of the frame Beatrix stuck a note to explain how it had been 'opened by me H.B. Heelis June 1936 in order to remove a chalk scribbled butterfly, seemingly done by a child, above the parrot. At the same time I put some work on lower part of parrot and door panels perhaps indiscreetly — The ducks [picture] which I did not open or touch is much the most finished ... This curious picture was bought for 50/- from Mr Allan antique dealer, Aspatria, Cumberland. I think it will be late 18th or early 19th century.'

The walls are hung with William Morris's 'Daisy' pattern wallpaper. As Beatrix said, the daisies are 'not suitable as a background for pictures in water-colours or prints, being a decoration in themselves, but for a background to my 4 poster nothing could be better'. She bought the paper direct from Morris & Co., and said it was printed from the original blocks. 'Morris & Co. make good reproductions.'

The mixture of the functional, the Oriental and the exotic is continued on the floor with a skin rug by the fire — not the lion-skin which was there in Beatrix's day, a Persian rug at the foot of the bed and a square of coir matting near the door — all as described as being in the room soon after Beatrix's death.

In 1934 William added the carved wooden lintel and shelf above the existing stone fireplace, inscribing the letters WHB and the date, to commemorate their twenty-first wedding anniversary.

LEFT *A corner of the bedroom showing William Morris's 'Daisy' pattern wallpaper. A lacquered cabinet on a stand painted with Chinese-style decoration sits next to one of a pair of tall cane-backed chairs, which Beatrix thought were Carolean. She said the 'turning of the stretchers is very good' and added 'they have Spanish feet'.*

RIGHT *Beyond the tester bed, hung with green hangings embroidered by Beatrix, the fireplace can be seen with its eighteenth-century plain stone surround, above which is the inscribed wooden lintel and shelf, added by William.*

Treasure Room

In this small room located in the centre of the front part of the house, called by Beatrix her treasure room (her cabinet of curiosities), she kept her miniature belongings as well as an eclectic mixture of pottery, porcelain, pictures and embroidery.

Her small curios are housed in an ebonized showcase. Arranged on its shelves are pieces of Wedgwood jasper and basaltware alongside a salt-glazed tea pot, a pair of spill vases decorated with a frieze of nymphs, Japanese ivory netsuke and heavily carved small cases, machine-turned boxes and odd items of jewellery such as marcazite and plastic beads. There is also a collection of miniature bronze figures of characters from her books, given to her by an Austrian admirer.

Above the showcase hangs an oil painting of the old ferry hotel on Windermere, 'bought at Miss Lily Heelis's sale July 28 1931, Hawkshead Hall, previous history unknown'. (Hawkshead Hall was where William Heelis lived before his marriage with the two spinster sisters of his partner.) Next to an ebonized cabinet inlaid with ivory is a rare tinsel picture. Dating from the early nineteenth

century, these black and white engravings of famous actors and actresses were sold to be decorated with stick-on pieces of glittery, foiled 'tinsel' paper. This one shows 'Mr Payne as Robin Hood' and was published in 1839. On another wall is a pair of Caldecott prints, one of a woman hanging washing in an orchard 'The pretty maid hanging out the clothes was the Caldecott's maid at the house in Surrey.'

Opposite the curio showcase is a dolls' house, not the one Beatrix used for *The Tale of Two Bad Mice*, but containing the plaster food that Hunca Munca and Tom Thumb stole.

LEFT *On either side of the painting of the Ferry Hotel on Windermere hang a pair of nineteenth-century oval flower studies of* Primula farinosa *and* Rosa gallica *by Valentine Bartholomew.*

RIGHT *On the mid-nineteenth century ebonized cabinet are pieces of Wedgwood jasper ware; to the right hangs the tinsel picture of Robin Hood.*

LEFT *Most of the furnishings and food in the dolls' house were bought from the London toy shop, Hamley's, by Beatrix's friend Norman Warne. She subsequently copied them for* The Tale of Two Bad Mice. *She wrote that 'the things will do beautifully; the ham's appearance is enough to cause indigestion'. The kitchen table and chairs, cutlery, saucepan, griddle, iron, bellows, dustpan and brush, tin hob-grate, bird-cage and plaster food in the dolls' house all appear in the book.*

BELOW *Hunca Munca trying to carve the ham in* The Tale of Two Bad Mice.

RIGHT ABOVE *Two Caldecott prints hang above the dolls' house. These are framed on either side by a pair of tapestry panels, said to have been embroidered by Beatrix on the frame in the sitting room.*

RIGHT BELOW *A shelf on top of the dolls' house is filled with shells, miniature fans and other dolls' accessories, arranged around Peter Rabbit's red and white spotted handkerchief.*

Sitting Room

In the third room at the front of the house, set out as a small sitting room, diagonally opposite the door to one side of the window is a chest of drawers on top of which stands a bedroom mirror. The combination of a chest with a mirror on top is one Beatrix had sketched at an old house in Winchelsea. The looking-glass with ivory knobs belonged to Beatrix's great-grandmother, Alice Crompton.

Opposite the fireplace is a mahogany square piano made in London in 1810 by Muzio, Clementi and Co. It might have come from one of the Heelis sales, for it is inscribed under the right lid with three sets of initials – M.H., E.H. and M.H. – and the dates 1838 and 1839.

Just inside the door stands a tall late eighteenth-century mahogany bureau bookcase filled with small pieces of china, some of which are souvenirs associated with her little books, such as a Wedgwood tea service portraying characters from her stories.

Around the walls are a selection of small oil paintings and a few watercolours including one entitled *Spring* by Beatrix and another by her brother Bertram, *Fields at Sunset*. Some of the oils, such as the coastal scene by Lord Leighton, probably came from her parents' collection, while the local view of the Langdale Pikes from Low Wood by James Francis Williams was more likely to have been bought by Beatrix.

RIGHT *Opening off the landing are doors to the sitting room, on the left, and to the treasure room, on the right. The floor is covered with wide oak boards, a feature of seventeenth- and early eighteenth-century Lake District houses. Just visible on the right is a corner of the 'Shropshire' blanket chest.*

LEFT *The final effect of this small sitting room was achieved only after Beatrix's death. She left instructions that the 'looking glass . . . and the small chest of drawers which it stands on' should be moved into this room from Castle Cottage. Above the fire is a nineteenth-century ornamental picture, View of a Lake, and on the shelf a pair of Derby porcelain vases. Beatrix's embroidery frame stands in front of the fireplace.*

LEFT *Above the square piano hangs an oil painting by Bertram Potter entitled* Fields at Sunset. *It is bound on the reverse with pages from* The Times Literary Supplement, *dated 1906.*

BELOW AND RIGHT *(Below) The 'Chippendale glass-fronted bureau', which Beatrix said was the first piece of antique furniture she ever bought; it was moved into the room from Castle Cottage after her death. (Right above) Grimwade Peter Rabbit children's ware with a 'pace-egg' decorated by Beatrix in the egg cup. Each Easter Sunday, local children decorated hard-boiled eggs and raced them down a hill. Beatrix always drew faces on some of these eggs. (Right centre) Staffordshire and Leedsware jugs, with Worcester and Copenhagen cups next to a Staffordshire fawn. (Right below) A Wedgwood tea service decorated with characters from the 'little books'.*

New Room

In the new wing she added on at the back of the house, Beatrix kept one room above the farmhouse kitchen for herself. This was the one she initially called her library and she used it to hang her brother Bertram's oil paintings. Bertram was six years her junior and, like her, had escaped from the confines of London life to become a farmer. He settled in Scotland but his life was not particularly happy. Scotland did not seem to give him lasting peace or satisfaction and he died from over-drinking in 1918 at the age of forty-six. His paintings reflect the somewhat melancholic side of his character. On the walls are four large landscape oils, rather grey in colour and showing untamed, boggy land-scapes of birch and willow, pine forests and dark canyons.

These pictures are rather squeezed into the room between a dado rail, a picture rail and a number of neo-classical pilasters. Around the door is the beginning of some egg-and-dart moulding carved into the woodwork which William started but never finished.

In one corner of the room is an oak bureau bookcase used by Beatrix for writing. Near by, from her grandmother's house, is one of the bentwood chairs which she used in some of her early drawings of mice spinning. The room now houses pieces from the small study she set up for herself at Troutbeck Park Farm: a red walnut bureau and three mahogany Chippendale-style chairs as well as a small cabinet full of curious china and glass.

LEFT *In the corner of the new room stands the oak bureau bookcase, dating from about 1825, which Beatrix used for writing. On top is a stuffed bittern. In front of the pilasters is a model of a three-mast schooner, probably made by a sailor. Ships of this type were built in the yards of Barrow-in-Furness in the 1880s and 1890s.*

BELOW *The view from the new room window, looking up Stoney Lane towards Moss Eccles Tarn above Near Sawrey —*
drawn by Beatrix for The Tale of Samuel Whiskers.

ABOVE *A cabinet, from Beatrix's study at Troutbeck Park Farm, filled with ruby glass and an assortment of porcelain including Chinese, Japanese, Crown Derby, Royal Worcester, Wedgwood, Copenhagen and Quimper ware.*

LEFT *The smaller cabinet houses carved ivory such as chess pieces, Japanese netsuke figures and densely carved oriental quill boxes.*

HILL TOP
GARDEN

ABOVE *The approach to the house is shown in enticing detail in the frontispiece for* The Tale of Tom Kitten.

LEFT *The garden in full bloom towards the end of June. The narrow, Brathay slate path leads up from the road and suddenly widens out to a gravelled yard in front of the house, with the dark recess of the porch at its centre.*

87

ALTHOUGH BEATRIX HAD NEVER GARDENED until she bought Hill Top, she had, as we have seen, taken an intense interest in plants and gardens from an early age. One of her earliest sketchbooks to survive, done at the age of eight, includes drawings of the garden at Dalguise. Between the ages of nine and ten she made numerous sketches of flowers such as foxgloves, pink campion, narcissi and orchids. As she grew older she continued to draw gardens visited on family holidays, such as Bedwell Lodge, Lingholm, Fawe Park and Lakefield. And then of course there were the gardens of her relatives at Melford Hall and Gwaynynog.

As with her depictions of interiors, she eschewed the grand, formal parts of the gardens, concentrating instead on working spaces, vegetable frames, greenhouses, walls, gates and beehives. With plants she focused on mixtures of productive and cottage garden plants, cabbages and roses, fruit trees and antirrhinums. She wrote far less about gardens than about the insides of houses. One of the few gardens she described in detail was the walled vegetable garden at Gwaynynog, which imprinted itself on her memory. '[It] is very large, two-thirds surrounded by a red-brick wall with many apricots, and an inner circle of old grey apple trees on wooden espaliers. It is very productive but not very tidy, the prettiest kind of garden, where bright old fashioned flowers grow amongst the currant bushes.' More than twenty years later the garden was reincarnated in two quite different ways: first as one of the main inspirations for her own garden at Hill Top and, even more memorably, as the background for *The Tale of The Flopsy Bunnies*.

When Beatrix bought Hill Top, the only garden was a small walled kitchen area opposite the front door, separated from the house by the farm track which then led down to the road. As soon as she had finished building her new wing in the summer of 1906, she turned her attention to the spaces outside. Within a few seasons, she

was to transform the surroundings of Hill Top into the luscious gardens that appear in *The Tale of Tom Kitten*.

First, she moved the drive away from the house, so creating a large space for her new garden between the new drive and the front of the house. 'Instead of the old winding road — with a tumble down wall covered with polypody [fern] — there is a straight wide road and very bare wall. Also heaps of soil everywhere and new railings', adding, somewhat apologetically, 'the new works though doubtless an improvement are painfully *new*'. The new drive, bordered with iron park railings, led from the road round the edge of the vegetable patch to the farm buildings and the Cannons' front door. She created a separate access path for her old part of the house along the line of the old drive, out through a small wicket gate in the wall beside the road.

Her new garden had four areas: the old kitchen garden, a large grass garth (paddock), a small orchard and a flower garden spanning the new pathway. However, it didn't all happen quite as planned. Arriving from London at the beginning of April, she discovered 'some work has been done all wrong, that I am a little vexed with. I started a man filling up one corner in the garden to make a flat lawn. I believe the word "tennis" *was* mentioned but I have never played it, so it conveyed nothing particular to my mind. I could not think why he was taking such a time and now I discover a thing big enough for playing football! Half the garden.' She decided enough was enough and no more wages should be spent on this part of the garden, arranging for the farmer to plant potatoes in it for the first year.

Quarrymen were brought in to make 'walks and beds'. They laid large irregular Brathay flags flat on the path and set others upright along the edges of the beds. They also built new high walls between the flower garden and the Tower Bank Arms, her immediate neighbour, and along one side of the vegetable garden. Sketches done by Beatrix of the farm, soon after she bought it, show the vegetable

FAR LEFT *Foxgloves and pink campion, drawn by Beatrix in 1876 when she was nine years old.*

LEFT *The long path in the vegetable garden at Gwaynynog, near Denbigh, with a stout trellis supporting espalier fruit trees behind the bed on the right. This view inspired Beatrix's designs for part of Hill Top garden.*

RIGHT *'Pace-eggers' photographed by Beatrix in the garden at Hill Top (date not known) not long after the new wall, path and beds were put in place. Each year the boys came begging for shillings with their mumming song: 'We've come a pace-eggin', I hope you prove kind . . .' (see p. 81).*

garden enclosed all round by low stone walls with a bee-bole, a shallow roofed recess for sheltering bee skeps, built into the wall nearest the house. She kept two of the walls, including the bee-bole, but replaced one wall with a hedge where it bordered the new drive. The fourth wall was rebuilt as a tall warm wall, with an outer skin of stone and inner facing of brick, all capped with large flat slates.

By July she was able, by chance, to populate the bee-bole. 'I found a swarm of bees on Sunday and caught them (it isn't quite so valiant as it sounds!), they were lying on the grass near the quarry, we think they had been out all night, and blown out of a tree; they were very numbed, but are all right now and a fine swarm. No one in the village has lost them, and I don't intend to inquire further afield! I have bought a box hive and Satterthwaite is fixing it up for me. I borrowed a straw "skep" to catch them in, and put it down over them.' The box hive still sits in the bee-bole – somewhat incongruously, as box hives do not need the shelter of bee-boles.

Most of the beds were ready for planting by mid-summer and she started to look for plants. She eyed up the roses at Lingholm where she was in August: 'there are some pretty roses, I wonder if they would carry'. It seems they wouldn't, but she did bring back some London pride, planting it as soon as she arrived at Hill Top; 'they look as if they quite enjoyed the change of climate'. Her cousin at Windermere sent over a hamper of big roots including Japanese anemones and sweet williams, which she thought would do 'nicely amongst the shrubs'.

Few opportunities for acquiring plants were passed by. The demolition of an old bridge at the bottom of Esthwaite provided some 'pretty wall-rue fern to plant in the garden wall', although she regretted the source: 'it is a pity to see it pulled down, I like old walls'. She used a visit to Windermere to good effect. '[I] impudently took a large

basket and trowel with me. She had the most untidy garden I ever saw. I got nice things in handfuls without any shame, amongst others a bundle of lavender slips, if they "strike" they will be enough for a lavender hedge; and another bundle of violet suckers, I am going to set some of them in the orchard.' In view of its name, it is ironic that some honesty was got even more deviously, stolen, as she put it, as 'it was put out to be burnt in a heap of garden refuse!', but she reconciled her action by Mrs Satterthwaite's comment that 'stolen plants always grow'.

Her need to fill the empty beds had quickly spread round the village, with the result that her planting times were soon being dictated by others. 'I have been planting hard all day — thanks to a well meant but slightly ill-timed present of saxifrage from Mrs Taylor at the corner cottage. She brought out a large newspaper full!' Beatrix thought the

LEFT *Photograph by Rupert Potter of Beatrix's planting to one side of the vegetable garden gate (date not known). Lilies, mossy saxifrage and* Primula japonica *can be seen.*

RIGHT *A view through the orchard towards the gate which leads on to Beatrix's new drive.*

FAR RIGHT *Keswick codling apples — a local variety — growing in the orchard. They were photographed by Beatrix (date not known).*

local saxifrage different from what she had known in London; it was 'longer in the stalk, more suitable for a rockery than for a flat surface'. 'I have had something from nearly every garden in the village', she wrote a short while later, adding, 'it is a time of year when there are clearances and bonfires — I am receiving half the "rubbish" in the village gardens . . .'

The planting was very carefully thought out. 'There is a quarryman who lives on the road to the ferry who has got some most splendid phloxes, they will look nice between the laurels while the laurels are small. I shall plant the lilies between the azaleas ... I have been busy planting cuttings of rock plants on the top of the garden wall — I have got cuttings of "white" rock which have crimson and purple flowers. I wonder if I shall ever get it to grow as well as Satterthwaite's.'

Other small rock and herbaceous plants came from begging round the village. Trees and shrubs, needed to give the garden some form, were bought from a nursery in Windermere. She planted lilac, rhododendron and 'red fuchsia, they say it will grow out of doors here all winter'.

It seems there were a few old apple trees in the garden when she bought the farm — 'the apples on the old trees prove to be very good cookers' — and to these she added more in her first autumn, writing the next spring that 'the little fruit trees are going to flower well, the first shower of rain will bring them out'. By 1910 she was enjoying harvesting her apples, pears and plums. Beneath the trees in the orchard the grass was carpeted with 'plenty of wild snowdrops' and to these were added the small, wild daffodils, or Lent lilies as they are known locally, which 'grow about Windermere', and indeed grow profusely all around the Lake District.

The planting provided an opportune moment for Beatrix to get involved in local politicking. It seems there were several local rows going on in the village but she was 'not in any of them at present – though much inclined!'. She was irritated by the fact that she was not getting her share of council manure and wondered about taking up the cudgels. 'I think I shall attack the county council about manure, I am entitled to all the road sweepings along my piece, and their old man is using it to fill up holes, which is both illegal and nasty.' It is not recorded whether she actually rose to the challenge, but a month later she was writing to explain how she was 'putting liquid manure on the apple trees!! It is a most interesting performance with a long scoop', illustrating the process with a tiny sketch of herself in a long skirt and hat wielding the scoop in front of a weeping manure heap.

Like the interior of the house, the garden was not something finished off quickly; rather it was a creation she worked on for many seasons, continually revisiting the planting and improving the layout as well as coping with the vagaries of the damp and cold Lake District weather. In 1908 she asked Warne to let her know how much she might expect to be paid as 'there is still ample opportunity to lay out the garden and surroundings'; in 1910 the severe wet

and stormy weather, when the 'lake had risen nearly a yard and my poor field of oats had been beaten flat', turned the garden into 'a perfect forest of groundsel ... it is easy to pull up which is a blessing'. But there was the benefit that 'the hollyhocks have been very good this year, they were about 12 to 14 feet high before the storm'.

Beatrix was not preserving a cottage garden; what she was doing was creating a garden – her own garden – in the cottage style. It was in this way that she conformed with what was then being written about gardens: the imagery of gardens, the way spaces within them should be divided up and above all how gardens should be seen as an extension of the buildings to which they belonged. Just a few years before, Gertude Jekyll had published her first hugely influential books on garden layout and planting, in which she advocated the use of 'old-fashioned' cottage garden

THIS PAGE AND OPPOSITE PAGE *From left to right: thalictrum; aquilegias; astrantia; geranium and fern; rambling roses; sea holly. Some plants thrive in the damp cool weather of the Lake District and these are the ones seen in many of the local gardens. Aquilegias, mallows, Welsh poppies, foxgloves and lady's mantle seed freely; ferns grow in abundance; geraniums like the shady skies; roses are more problematic and look good only when the summer is sunnier than usual.*

plants, mixed borders planted with a profusion of colour, all within a controlled and human-scale setting, linked in various ways to the ambience of the house.

William Morris, too, was helping to shape the prevailing emerging fashion for old-fashioned plants, formal arrangements of spaces, rustic trellises, weathered stone walls and gardens that merged imperceptibly into the houses. A garden, he said, should be both 'orderly and rich. It should be well fenced off from the outside world. It should by no means imitate the wilfulness or wildness of nature, but should look like a thing never to be seen except near a house. It should look like part of the house.'

Morris and Jekyll directed much of their early attention to large gardens, but in the decade after 1900 there was also a good deal of informed interest in, and study of, traditional cottage gardens. Some writers argued that the plants and layout of cottage gardens could at times be seen as miniature versions of grander, baroque gardens, where paths and small hedges divide up the spaces into densely planted formal beds. Traditional cottage gardens were analysed, described and painted. Some of the most evocative are Helen Allingham's illustrations in which the cottages are just visible behind tight clusters of tall flowers and rampant climbers. Stewart Dick, writing on the ideal

cottage garden in his book *Cottage Homes of England*, published in 1909 and illustrated by Allingham, said: 'In its small space it contains so much. Flowers in profusion everywhere. Roses tended with loving care ... tall holly-hocks reaching almost to the ... eaves, sweet smelling wallflowers spreading their fragrance far into the dusty road. Pansies ... and in their season, snowdrops, crocuses, primrose and violet ..., a row or two of peas and beans, turnips, carrots, lettuce, cabbage and cauliflower, and a patch of rhubarb, with its great spreading leaves, in the corner by the hedge ... You do not look for rarities in the cottager's garden, just the sweet, homely flowers, and the wholesome vegetables.'

Jekyll, Morris and others took the essence of these gardens and used it to underpin new garden design. Cottage gardens may look unplanned and 'wild'; in reality they were very tightly planned and controlled, as Jekyll understood. She advocated a pleasurable confusion of leaves and flowers spilling out of a carefully planned framework. In partnership with the architect Edwin Lutyens, Jekyll suggested how this framework of spaces could be created by the use of architectural features such as walls, paths, pergolas and trellises constructed out of local materials. They also went on to champion the use of 'antiques', specially collected pieces of statuary or furniture, to highlight a

particular area of the garden — an extension of the concept of treasures collected for indoors.

With its careful division into several, quite intimate areas — the vegetable garden, the flower borders flanking the path, the grass garth and the small orchard — Hill Top reflects these precepts well. The partition of the vegetable garden was made with a raised brick-lined wall which separated it from the grass garth and also from the flower borders either side of the path. Another visual divide was created by the construction of a stout trellis of oak, for espalier fruit trees

ABOVE *Beatrix, under the old Scots pine near the small gate which leads on to the road, photographed by Rupert Potter in May 1913. The tree was felled for safety reasons in 1992 and a replacement is now growing up. Little is growing in the garden — spring often comes late in the Lake District.*

RIGHT *The garden is usually in its full glory in early July. Thalictrums, lychnis, chalcedonica, alliums, foxgloves, sedums, acanthus, lupins, astrantias, Canterbury bells and sweet peas fight for space. Later in the year some of these give way to Michaelmas daisies, lemon balm and self-sown angelica. In the spring lilac, azaleas, irises, honesty, Turks-head lilies, peonies and sweet williams make a good show together with ripe red gooseberries.*

at the back of the deep border against the garth. The narrowness of the paths and the gated openings emphasized the small scale of the spaces. The 'rustic' nature of the garden was reflected in the use of local materials: rough, uneven flags for the path, thick oak planks for the trellis (which was topped with turned acorns) and local quarried stone for the new walls.

RIGHT *The stout oak fence with its ostrich-egg finials, set parallel to the slate path, is similar to one Beatrix sketched in the garden at Gwaynynog, Denbigh.*

BELOW *The kittens on the wall in* The Tale of Tom Kitten. *Polypody ferns, which thrive in damp weather and are quite a feature of the old dry-stone walls of the Lake Distict, are growing in between the stones of the wall.*

One strong direct influence on Beatrix in carving out her new spaces was clearly the garden at Gwaynynog. A sketch she did there, of a long straight path dipping slightly into the distance, bordered by deep beds enclosed on one side by a trellis, is almost exactly the view she created looking from the door of Hill Top down the path towards the road. Only the scale is different: the large walled garden at Gwaynynog has shrunk to cottage garden size.

Beatrix did not introduce 'antiques' into her garden, but she included some surprising exotics. Planting rhododendrons and azaleas, definitely not cottage garden plants, as well as some of the newly discovered primulas seems to have been her way of introducing treasures. She also planted a grape vine against the warm brick wall, sheltering it with a glass pentice supported on iron brackets. By 1910 the vine bore fruit. 'I have got 3 bunches ... but I doubt if they will ever ripen out of doors.'

At Castle Cottage, Beatrix also created a garden, fencing off a piece from the sloping field in front of the house. Since her death the garden has been much altered and is no longer as she described it the summer of 1924. 'I have lots of flowers, I am very fond of my garden, it is irregular old fashioned farm garden, with a box hedge round the flower bed, and moss roses and pansies and black currants and strawberries and peas — and big sage bushes for Jemima, but onions always do badly. I have tall white bell flowers I am fond of, they are just going over, next there will be phlox; and last come the michaelmas daisies and chrysanthemums. Then soon after Christmas we have snowdrops, they grow wild and come up all over the garden and orchard, and in some of the woods.'

Looking down the path towards the road. The oak fence on the right of the deep border is barely visible. The planting is a happy profusion of flowers, herbs, fruit and vegetables. Chives, camomile and thyme perch on the edge of the bed; geraniums and lettuce sit between the taller acanthus, globe thistles, lemon verbena, lilies and sweet peas and, wherever there is space, lady's mantle and Welsh poppies find a footing. On the left a flowering cherry hangs over the path.

SAWREY TALES

LEFT *Beatrix's watercolour of* Sawrey under Snow *painted on 7 March 1909 from a path at the back of Hill Top. A typical Lake District chimneypot is clearly shown on Buckle Yeat Cottage in the centre of the picture, formed from five slates, four around the sides and one on top held in position with a small stone weight.*

ABOVE *Near Sawrey from the east. In the foreground are three cottages known as the Castle and, in the background on the left, is the Tower Bank Arms immediately in front of Hill Top.*

THE FIRST EIGHT YEARS of Beatrix's ownership of Hill Top, when she made frequent visits from London, were her most productive period as a writer. Nine of the 'little books' published in rapid succession between 1905 and 1913 are set in and around the farm. Hill Top seems to have been the key that unlocked tales roughed out in her sketchbooks many years before.

Looking over Hill Top and Near Sawrey from the hill to the south of Hill Top. The large house, near the centre of the picture, is Tower Bank House, which Beatrix agreed to buy just before she died.

The first Sawrey tale to appear was *The Tale of The Pie and The Patty-Pan,* which she had written two years before she bought Hill Top and which she now re-set in the village. Ribby the cat seems to have been one of the Hill Top cats, while 'the little dog called Duchess' belonged to the gardener at Ees Wyke. In the story, Ribby lives in the gardener's house, which is based on one of three Lakefield cottages near Ees Wyke, where Beatrix sketched the stone-flagged larder with its tiny window, shelves full of bread crocks and boxes of apples, and also a swill basket – a local oval-shaped shallow basket made from plaited shavings of oak. The Duchess is given as her home Buckle Yeat Cottage, then the Post Office in the centre of the village, which had a particularly pretty cottage garden shown in all its exuberance in the book. Hill Top appears in the frontispiece, seen across the fields as it was when Beatrix bought it, still with its whitewashed walls and timber woodshed.

The interiors of these two cottages are recorded in minute detail in the tale, and the pictures are a wonderful record of now-vanished cottage life. On the mantelshelf above the range stand tea caddies; a bunch of herbs hangs from the ceiling; a plump cushion softens the stiffly upholstered Victorian chaise longue; and the window ledge houses rows of potted plants, geraniums, Christmas cacti and campanulas.

LEFT *The luscious garden of Buckle Yeat Cottage, painted in about 1905 as a background sketch for* The Tale of The Pie and The Patty-Pan. *At the side of the garden is a 'shard' fence, formed from large interlocking pieces of local stone.*

RIGHT ABOVE *Buckle Yeat Cottage today.*

RIGHT CENTRE *One of eleven drawings Beatrix did inside Mrs Lord's cottage at Lakefield, Near Sawrey, in 1902. The potted plants stand in front of a sash window with particularly tiny panes of glass.*

RIGHT BELOW *Looking towards Esthwaite Water from fields near Ees Wyke.*

Her next story, *The Tale of Mr. Jeremy Fisher*, had been in the making for even longer. It was first hinted at in a story-letter to Noel Moore in 1893, beginning 'once upon a time there was a frog called Jeremy Fisher, and he lived in a little house on the banks of the river ...' The letter was written from Scotland and the river was the Tay. In the finished story his lily-leaf boat lives on a pond. The pond she illustrates seems to combine the tall reeds around the edge of Esthwaite Water, visible from the hill above Hill Top, with elements of Moss Eccles Tarn, a small stretch of water on Hill Top farmland high above Sawrey. Beatrix and William kept a small boat there and she herself planted the waterlilies which intersperse the reeds in the story.

LEFT *The dawn mist lifts over Esthwaite Water — in the distance to the north lies Hawkshead; on the left of the picture are the peaks of the Langdale Pikes.*

ABOVE *Esthwaite Water and the Langdale Pikes in* The Tale of Mr. Jeremy Fisher.

A new kitten at Belle Green, where Beatrix stayed when she purchased Hill Top, was the inspiration for her next Sawrey book, *The Tale of Tom Kitten*. The kitten became Tom Kitten's mother, Tabitha Twitchit, while Tom himself was based on earlier drawings she had done of a Windermere mason's cat. Beatrix used the book to show off her new garden in all its crowded glory — or more accurately how she hoped it would look once it had matured. The cats are shown advancing up the new path to the house alongside her deep flower border with its mass of cottage garden flowers such as pinks, pansies, forget-me-nots and day lilies, along with soft fruit bushes and espalier apples on a thick trellis. The porch is swathed in roses and clematis. Alongside the road the old stone wall, where the three kittens are found, is clothed in moss and polypody ferns.

The Tale of Jemima Puddle-Duck provided an opportunity to distil the essence of her new farming life, which began when she bought Hill Top and helped the Cannons to farm it. Beatrix turned her attention to the farm and Mrs Cannon's practice of raising ducklings by getting a hen to sit on the duck eggs. In the book we see the Cannons' small son removing eggs from under the rhubarb leaves in the kitchen garden; the farm sheep-dog, Kep; the farm cart and boskins (divisions for the cow stalls) in the old barn; the farmyard after Beatrix's alterations; and a charcoal burner's hut. She had seen the conical thatched hut in the autumn of 1906 on the far side of Esthwaite Water where charcoal was being burnt 'like a smouldering volcano' for the gunpowder works. It is of course used to house the villain of the tale, the sandy-whiskered gentleman. The story also contains some of her most memorable drawings of the landscape around Hill Top, such as the misty views of Esthwaite Water from the hill above the farm and woods full of foxgloves.

Beatrix's growing fascination with the Hill Top cats — bought by the Cannons to try to turn back what seemed like an army of rats — provided the basis for what is perhaps her masterpiece, *The Tale of Samuel Whiskers*. The story allowed her to celebrate her own creation, the transformation of Hill Top.

When she had first brought in the local builder to look at the structure of her new house, he had broken through into the large old chimney of the hall, 'burrowed into the back of it this morning without any downfall, thank goodness. It is also four foot thick, and full of chaff and hay pulled in by the rats . . .' This large, cavernous space up the chimney, the lair of the rats, is the one discovered by Tom Kitten. From it he falls into the attic space and is tied up by Samuel Whiskers and his wife, Anna Maria. As Tabitha Twitchit searches for her errant son, on the staircase, in the attic, inside an oak chest, the rooms are shown in mesmerizing detail. The rats are seen scurrying across the hall in front of the dresser towards the foot of the stairs and then rolling their rolling pin across the landing. When the rats are finally driven out of Hill Top they are shown on the run through the village, watched by Beatrix in the background. At last they take refuge in the barn of Farmer Potatoes, who was in reality Farmer Postlethwaite, one of Beatrix's near neighbours.

ABOVE *Jemima sets off on a fine spring afternoon along the cart track behind Hill Top farm in* The Tale of Jemima Puddle-Duck.

OPPOSITE LEFT *A watercolour sketch of John Taylor's shop in Near Sawrey for* The Tale of Ginger and Pickles.

OPPOSITE RIGHT *Mr Tod peering through the hinges of the half-open bedroom door in* The Tale of Mr. Tod.

The Tale of Mr. Tod celebrates the wider landscape of Near Sawrey. Mr Tod, the fox, has a house at the top of Bull Banks, under Oatmeal Crag, where Beatrix had sat and mused many years before. There are long views around the edge of a rather wintry Esthwaite Water. The interior of Mr Tod's home provided another opportunity: to present enticing details of the interiors of village houses. In the frontispiece, Mr Tod is shown standing on a stone flag floor against a timber plank wall covered with thick layers of sage-green limewash. The wall is clearly of muntin and plank construction, the name given to a common local construction of interlocking thick and thin vertical planks. Tea caddies adorn the mantelpiece in Mr Tod's kitchen, while blue and white willow-pattern china and a squat silver salt are laid on a crisp white tablecloth over the kitchen table. The beehive-shaped brick oven, next to the range, drawn from one at the Sun Inn in Hawkshead, is used in the story as somewhere for Brock the badger to imprison the kittens.

The inspiration for *The Tale of Ginger and Pickles* was the village shop set at the corner of Smithy Lane and the main road through Near Sawrey, run by John Taylor, a joiner, then bedridden, and his wife and daughter. In the book Ginger the cat and his terrier friend Pickles keep shop. Most of the interiors seem to have been copied from sketches Beatrix did inside the Near Sawrey shop but other houses from the village also appear as does the Corner Shop in Hawkshead. Beatrix wrote how the book caused amusement: 'It has got a good many views which can be recognised in the village which is what they like, they are all quite jealous of each others houses and cats getting into a book.' It was dedicated to John Taylor, who '"thinks he might pass as a dormouse!" (three years in bed and never a grumble!)'.

Beatrix's last Sawrey story, *The Tale of Pigling Bland*, was, as Graham Greene once commented, 'the nearest Miss Potter had approached to a conventional love story'. As is the case with several of her other stories, this one had been planned for some time. It was based on her prize-winning pigs and in particular a small, black girl-pig, Pig-wig, bought from a neighbouring farmer against the wishes of John Cannon. Three years before the book was published she wrote about how she 'spent a very wet hour *inside* the pig stye drawing the pigs'.

We see distant views of Sawrey's 'peaceful green valleys, where little white cottages nestled in gardens and orchards, "That's Westmorland," said Pig-wig', and two pigs walking away from the crossroads between Hill Top and Esthwaite Water. The model for the kitchen in the book was Spout House in Far Sawrey, the neighbouring village to Near Sawrey, although Pig-wig is shown in the kitchen sitting on a high-backed chair next to a dresser which is clearly the one at Hill Top.

Although Beatrix denied that it was a portrait of her and William, the flight of the two pigs at the end of the story 'over the hills and far away!' seems to symbolize the journey Beatrix was about to take from her old life of writer and artist to her new role as Mrs William Heelis, Lake District farmer. With her marriage her creative energies began to be channelled in new directions. Over the next thirty years she only produced a few more books.

LEFT *'That's Westmorland . . . ', from* The Tale of Pigling Bland. *In the story Pigling crosses over Brathay Bridge into Lancashire and then returns over Colwith Bridge to live in Westmorland.*

RIGHT *View from the top of Tilberthwaite quarries over part of the Monk Coniston estate. Beyond the green fields is High Tilberthwaite Farm and on the left Low Tilberthwaite Cottages, built for quarry workers. Holme Ground Farm is hidden in the trees on the right.*

FARMING LIFE

LEFT *Hill Top Farm approached along the new road. The pigsties and dairy buildings to the left and the pentice roof on the barn were added by Beatrix.*

ABOVE *Jemima is escorted back to Hill Top Farm in* The Tale of Jemima Puddle-Duck.

IT IS DIFFICULT TO KNOW whether Beatrix ever imagined that her life would change so drastically and that she would become a landowner of a huge estate and a campaigner for the conservation of the Lake District. But with the benefit of hindsight, the stages of her life can be seen to have had a logical progression. Her drawings led her to want to live in the countryside that formed the background to her stories; in living there she wanted to be part of the farming way of life; in turn this led to her concern for its vulnerability and to her desire to save it from what she saw as despoliation. And so, the shy girl, with an intense interest in the minutiae of life and the world of the imagination, grew and developed to command larger canvases, first one small farm, then two and three, and finally whole tracts of the countryside where real transformation could be accomplished.

During the first ten years after her marriage to William, when she lived at Castle Cottage and helped the Cannons farm the land at Hill Top, she soon formed strong opinions on the routines of farming life and also saw opportunities for improvement: 'I have been discussing salt butter with Mrs Cannon, they don't seem to use it in this [part of the] country, but I think it ought to answer; it is quite time butter went up [in price], it is still only 1/1 or 1/2 a pound.'

Her interest in farming was not sentimental. Only three years after buying Hill Top her attention was taken by what she saw as 'grandmotherly' legislation to protect the young from the perceived cruelty of farming ways and she drafted a letter of protest: 'it has become illegal for a "child" under 16 years of age to be present at the slaughter and cutting up of carcasses ... do our rulers seriously maintain that a farm-lad of 15½ years must not assist at the cutting-up? One of the interesting reminiscences of my early years is the memory of helping to scrape the smiling countenance of my grandmother's deceased pig with scalding water and the sharp-edged bottom of a brass candle-stick ... Lord Rosebery is right. The present generation is being reared upon tea — and slops.' (Lord Rosebery was Prime Minister from 1894–5 and presumably at this time was voicing his disquiet at the attitudes of the young, as he did on the state of politics.)

FARMING LIFE

Her concerns quickly became more local and her methods more wide-ranging. In 1912, she turned her attention to threats posed by flying boats, which were to be built in a factory on the eastern shore of Windermere. She was concerned at the 'danger, turmoil and possible pecuniary damage' to animals crossing on the Windermere ferry in that 'ramshackle, picturesque boat, heavy-laden with ... the carrier's tilt cart and bustling motor, or homely toppling loads of oak bark and hoopers' swills, or droves of sheep and cattle'. She sent a letter of protest about the noise of the hydroplane, which she likened to 'millions of bluebottles, plus a steam-threshing engine', to *Country Life*. A petition soon followed with a call to drive the flying boats off the lake and she approached doctors, nurses, farmers and publishers to support it, signing herself Beatrix Potter to publishers whom she thought knew her as an author and 'H.B. Potter, *farmer*', to locals and the farming community. Her campaign was entirely successful and by the end of the year a government enquiry resulted in the closure of the factory.

This campaign, and the success of it, reflected growing concern at threats to the peace and beauty of the Lake District, as well as the determination shown by a few people such as Beatrix to try and stem the tide through self-help actions. She was joining a long line of distinguished residents of the Lake District, including poets William Wordsworth and Robert Southey, and John Ruskin, who had all campaigned to stop what they saw as the despoliation of their chosen home by 'oft-comers'. The trickle of tourists who ventured into the area in the second half of the eighteenth century had turned to a flood by the end of the nineteenth century. The tourists had brought in their wake developers only too anxious to cater for the visitors' needs. The Lake District was coming under threat from hotels and villas, aeroplane factories and a host of other new interventions that many saw as changing the character of the area for the worse. But this popularity brought with it

the seeds of its salvation, as many of those who visited felt strongly enough to do something about it. Of the signatories for Beatrix's campaign against flying boats, thirty-four came from doctors and nurses at a hospital in London.

Beatrix's campaign was one of a host of other local initiatives to stop development and support the retention of open spaces in the first twenty years of the twentieth century. The catalyst for much of this action was the National Trust, which had been founded in 1895 as a national organization to hold land for the benefit of the nation. One of the Trust's three founders, and its Honorary Secretary, was Beatrix's friend Canon Rawnsley, then vicar of Crosthwaite near Keswick, who fought tirelessly to keep open footpaths and stop lake-shore development and who had founded the Lake District Defence Society in 1883.

In 1923 Beatrix was able to take direct action on her own to stop development when the spectacularly sited Troutbeck Park Farm, with its fine seventeenth-century farmhouse and bank barns, came up for sale and was attracting interest from developers who wanted to put houses on the bottom land near Troutbeck village. By this time she had had twenty-five 'little books' published and their income allowed her to move from being a small-scale farmer to becoming much more of a substantial landowner. She bought outright the dramatic farm of 1,500 acres with its grazing land sweeping up to the lower slopes of the Kirkstone Pass to the north and its large, prominent, south-facing whitewashed farmhouse set against the slopes of the 'Tongue', a knoll that divides the forking valley.

Troutbeck Park Farm, seen from near the road heading up to the Kirkstone Pass. Behind the farm is Troutbeck Tongue and beyond the fell. Beatrix wrote: 'Troutbeck Tongue is uncanny; a place of silence and whispering echoes. It is a mighty table-land between two streams. They rise together north of the Tongue, in one maze of bogs and pools . . .' Shortly before her death she recalled how she 'loved to wander on the Troutbeck Fell . . . more often I went alone. But never lonely. There was the company of gentle sheep, and wild flowers and singing waters.'

Troutbeck Park Farm was in a very run-down state. A neighbour later recalled Beatrix saying that when she followed the Coniston foxhounds across the Park's land and waded through the beck (the local word for stream), taking off her shoes and stockings, the beck was the only clean place on the farm. Almost immediately after she purchased it she drafted a will leaving the farm to the National Trust. Two years later, she set out precisely how the Trust should manage the farm when she died, summing up traditional Lake District farming practices in the process. In her instructions, she showed a keen eye for the details of Lake District husbandry and landscape, tempered with characteristic practicality and decisiveness.

A particular concern of hers was sheepstock, on which she wrote: 'At present I am minded to fix the number of "landlord's stock sheep" at the number of 1100 sheep viz. 700 ewes, 180 twinters, 220 hogs — all to be purebred heafed Herdwicks.' Twinters are sheep in their second winter and hogs are young sheep in their first winter. Herdwick sheep are only found in the high fells of the Lake District. They have the unusual attribute of becoming 'heafed' or 'hefted' to the fell on which they were weaned, which means they will always return, not just to the same fell, but to the same part of the fell. When farm tenancies change, the local tradition (which still applies today) is that those sheep heafed to the fell, over which the farm has grazing rights, are transferred with the farm as the landlord's flock.

Herdwick sheep are very hardy and ideally suited to the harsh weather of the Lakeland fells. Their lambs are small and lean and their wool coarse and grey. Even in 1900 the Herdwick breed was under threat as more farmers turned to keeping breeds with softer fleeces and plumper lambs in response to changing demands from the woollen and meat industries. In an effort to try and revive this local breed, in 1899, just four years after he helped form the National Trust, Canon Rawnsley founded the Herdwick Sheep Breeders' Association to encourage interest in these sheep and to try to re-establish them as viable farming products. On her farms, Beatrix was able to try and put Rawnsley's ideas into practice.

When Beatrix bought Troutbeck Park Farm it was tenanted. Three years later the tenant left and she decided to run the farm herself with the help of a shepherd. The man she chose was Tom Storey, then working at Townend Farm further down the Troutbeck valley. Tom was a Herdwick man and with his help — and the help of a newly introduced cure for sheep-fluke (fluke was a disease which plagued sheep) — Beatrix built up a celebrated flock of Herdwick sheep at the farm.

Entering her Herdwicks for local competitive shows, she quickly became a familiar figure. Soon she was invited to be a judge. In 1929 she wrote with pride: 'We have taken a number of first prizes this summer with the sheep — at all the local shows; and I think we could have gone to the "Royal" as we beat Willie Wilson with lambs yesterday at Ennerdale, and he has held the field for many seasons as

OPPOSITE ABOVE *Study by Beatrix of a Herdwick sheep's head (date not known).*

OPPOSITE BELOW *Close-up of a Herdwick ram. The lambs are born with very dark brown fleeces; as they grow older the fleeces turn a light grey colour.*

RIGHT *Beatrix, Tom Storey and a prize-winning Herdwick ewe at a Lake District show (date not known).*

BELOW *Prize cups and certificates, which Beatrix won for sheep exhibited at local shows, are housed in her husband's old offices — now the Beatrix Potter Gallery.*

prominence the farm has had since it was part of a medieval deer park. The present house dates from the seventeenth century and has circular chimneys (a feature of the Troutbeck valley), an arched porch and a slate drip-course above the lower windows. Troutbeck Park Farm gave Beatrix the opportunity to be her own architect when she designed and had built a new house for a shepherd next to the main farmhouse. This was a very assured piece of work: the house sits happily in its own garth (paddock) and in its architectural details mimics the main house. One gains the impression that Beatrix much enjoyed this exercise. Inside the house she commemorated her achievement with a datestone on the fireplace lintel.

Beatrix used Troutbeck Park Farm as a setting for her story *The Fairy Caravan*, written for an American publisher. In later life she recalled walks to the old barns west of the farmhouse, which had once been part of a separate, small farm, called High House: 'there was an old barn there that we call High Buildings. It is never used except sometimes by shepherds, and when I was younger and used to take long walks, I used to eat my bread and cheese at High Buildings, or shelter from the rain. That was where the Caravan sheltered in a very wild rainstorm, and Xarifa made acquaintance with the melancholy Mouse.'

By the mid-1920s, Hill Top and Castle Cottage had become objects of pilgrimage for some of Beatrix's

Herdwick king.' As her friend the artist Delmar Banner recalled after her death: 'At all sheep shows could be seen her short, stout, venerable figure, her countenance full of intelligence and humour, her plump, apple-rosy cheeks, and shrewd blue eyes.'

Between 1930 and 1938 she won all the prizes for Herdwick ewes at Keswick, Ennerdale, Eskdale, Loweswater and at many other local shows. 'We had speeches at lunch, at the Hawkshead Agricultural Show, and an old jolly farmer – replying to a "toast" – likened me – the president – to the first prize cow! He said she was a lady-like animal; and one of us had neat legs, and walked well; but I think that was the cow not me, being slightly lame.'

She kept up her association with the Herdwick Sheep-breeders' Association. 'I am in the chair at the Herdwick Breeders' Association meetings. You would laugh to see me, amongst the other farmers – usually in a tavern (!) after a sheep fair. We are serious enough, about the future.' Shortly before her death she was elected President of the Association but did not live to take up the office.

The farmhouse at Troutbeck Park Farm is a substantial building, much larger than Hill Top. This reflects the

ABOVE *The main farmhouse at Troutbeck Park Farm, as Beatrix drew it for* The Fairy Caravan, 1929. *She used some artist's licence, saying that 'the shelf is not really there, with bee hives'.*

OPPOSITE *Beatrix used drawings of her pet, long-haired guinea-pigs for* The Fairy Caravan. *This is an earlier drawing of a guinea-pig for* Appley Dapply's Nursery Rhymes, 1917.

American admirers. Beatrix quickly discovered she liked the 'nice Americans' and felt relaxed in their company. 'I am always pleased to see Americans, I don't know what I think of you as a nation (with a big N) but the individuals who have looked for Peter Rabbit have all been delightful.' They shared her appreciation of 'memories of old times, the simple country pleasures, the old farmhouse, the sublime beauty of the lonely hills', her furniture, china and 'treasures' and above all her growing enthusiasm for conservation. She found them easy to correspond with and began lengthy exchanges of letters with, amongst others, Anne Carroll Moore, the children's librarian at the New York Public Library, and Bertha Mahoney of the Boston Bookshop.

When, in 1927, Cockshott Point (a prominent piece of shoreline on the east side of Windermere) came under threat of development and a group of local people set about raising money for its purchase by the National Trust, Beatrix had no hesitation in May in writing to her Boston friends to mobilize support, nor in producing fifty drawings copied from four of the original illustrations for Peter Rabbit: 'Peter Rabbit is not begging for himself — and he offers something. Beatrix Potter has very much at heart an appeal to raise a fund to save a strip of fore shore, woodland and meadow near Windermere ferry from imminent risk of disfigurement by extensive building and town extension. So many nice and kind Americans come through the Lake District on their tour, some of them ask after Peter Rabbit. Do you think any of them would give a guinea (our £1.1.0) to help this fund, in return for an autographed drawing?'

By November she had raised £100, entered in the Cockshott Point subscription list as being from friends in Boston. Beatrix wrote with

satisfaction the following spring: 'the glebe land estate is quite secure now: ... and it will be thrown open to the public next summer — to the great pleasure of strangers from the Lancashire mill towns who like to picnic beside the Lake'.

Her friendship with Americans, and in particular with a Mrs J. Templeman Coolidge and her son Henry P., from Boston, encouraged Beatrix to start writing again. After one visit to Hill Top, during which Beatrix had told Henry P. that she was having trouble in getting a guinea-pig to use as a model, the Coolidges stopped at Harrods on their way back through London and despatched to Hill Top two long-haired guinea-pigs. Beatrix sent short stories about the guinea-pigs to Henry P. and, following a visit from Alexander McKay, an American publisher, she was persuaded to put the stories into book form. Despite many misgivings that she would not be able to do the illustrations to her satisfaction — 'my eyes have lost the faculty of seeing clean colours' — the book *The Fairy Caravan* was published in America in 1929. It was followed in 1930 by *The Tale of Little Pig Robinson*. The royalties from these two books came at an opportune moment. The five years of economic downturn from 1925 had hit Lake District farmers hard. As the depression took hold, it also threatened the landscape, as land prices began to fall to levels developers could afford. The core of the Lake District with its small farms and network of stone walls, reflecting an agricultural tradition that had persisted since medieval times, was becoming ever more vulnerable. This was the threat Beatrix was responding to when she bought Troutbeck Park Farm. In 1929 when the Monk Coniston estate — 2,550 acres of land around the head of Coniston Water — was put on the market the threat had reached a much larger scale.

The Monk Coniston estate had been built up by James Garth Marshall in and after 1836. It consisted of the well-known beauty spot of Tarn Hows, lakes and conifer planting laid out as a pleasure ground for Monk Coniston Hall (the Marshalls' house), seven farms including High and Low Yewdale, Yew Tree, High and Low Tilberthwaite and Holme Ground, as well as cottages, quarries and open fell land. Beatrix heard about the sale from her husband and immediately alerted the National Trust. 'After dinner, Mr Heelis and I are going to Coniston. There is a lovely stretch of mountain and valley to sell there ... I am very interested because my great grandfather had land there and I always longed to buy it back and give it to the Trust in remembrance.'

Her great-grandfather was Abraham Crompton, 1757–1829, who lived first at Chorley Hall at Chorley and then at Lune Villa, both in Lancashire. Like his son, Edmund, he was in the textile business. He bought Holme Ground Farm at Tilberthwaite in 1810, and kept it until his death.

It seems he let out the farm to a tenant and used the larger of the two farmhouses for weekends and holidays. Holme Ground House, as it is now known, is set against the backdrop of Holme Fell and looks east down the Tilberthwaite valley. It is by no means a typical farmhouse, having been remodelled, perhaps by Abraham Crompton, in the early nineteenth century, and now has quite lofty rooms and sash windows arranged symmetrically around a pretty timber porch. In the mid-nineteenth century it had been bought by James Marshall, whose son was now selling.

Beatrix wrote to the National Trust to say she was interested in buying the Monk Coniston estate but 'I will say at once I cannot afford to present anything to the Trust, much as it would please me to do so – because this speculation means selling out what is the main stay of my income [her investments] and replacing it by rent.' She went on to add though 'except anything I collect in the U.S.A. and *that* I have earmarked for old Abraham's land'.

The Trust invited her to negotiate on their behalf. It was soon discovered that building was not the only threat and that there was a real danger that the land could be afforested: 'There may have been a disaster. Mr Marshall is afraid his London solicitor, Mr Owen, has sold the whole to the Forestry Commissioners ... have you any means of approaching the Forestry Commissioners? To try and get the valleys ... Perhaps Tilberthwaite Fell and Holme Fell and Tom Craggs would not matter, no great disfigurement by planting. But it would be a terrible pity to do away with the little green farms and to cut down the remaining scrubby timber.'

Beatrix was soon writing daily letters to the National Trust as the prolonged and tortuous negotiations with the Marshalls progressed. 'To the best of my belief "Jimmy" has sold to both parties. The result remains uncertain.

THIS PAGE AND OPPOSITE PAGE *Farms and cottages given, sold or bequeathed to the National Trust by Beatrix. From left to right: Holme Ground Farm, 'old Abraham's land', which Beatrix gave to the National Trust; Low Tilberthwaite Farm and Tilberthwaite Cottages, from Horse Crag; High Tilberthwaite Farm, from the path leading to Little Langdale; Waterhead Cottages, from Monk Coniston Hall grounds; Low Hallgarth, Little Langdale, seen from across Little Langdale Tarn; Rose Castle, at the edge of Tarn Hows.*

We may all end up in a lunatic asylum.' At times, Beatrix seemed to trust neither her husband, who was acting for her, nor the Marshalls' agent, Mr MacVey, whom she described as a 'fat little man lately promoted from selling furniture'. 'Mr MacVey's latest appearance here – accompanied by thunder and lightning at 9.30pm – announced that Mrs Jimmy, ... and her husband had accepted his terms subject to remarkable conditions; (I was listening behind the dining room door) one was that he and his stepson should hatch trout for two generations (trout or stepsons?) in the private water supply of Monk Coniston house which he has sold to a man he has quarrelled with ... you may have to fight it out with the foresters "pull d[evil], pull baker" [a reference to a tug of war shown in puppet shows].'

Finally the complex negotiations were successful and the Marshalls agreed to sell the whole estate to Beatrix, who funded the purchase mainly from her American book sales. She in turn agreed to sell on half to the National Trust once they had raised the funds. Surprisingly Beatrix chose to hand over to the Trust 'old Abraham's land', Holme Ground Farm; it seems it went as a gift rather than part of the sale. 'I have been much gratified to get back the piece of land in Tilberthwaite that belonged to my great-grandfather Abraham Crompton. I should have liked to

keep it for my lifetime, but on the whole it seemed wiser to make a gift of it to the National Trust when they bought the surrounding property.'

Once negotiations with the Trust were completed, Beatrix showed how astute she had become in her financial dealings since the early days of her Hill Top purchase: 'Perhaps you do not realise that I got back three quarters of the original purchase money of Monk Coniston while I kept the more valuable half of the estate ... as I took the initial risk I was entitled to reap any advantage.'

At the age of sixty-five, Beatrix found herself the owner of nearly 3,000 acres of the most significant landscape of the central Lakes. And as if managing all her own holding was not enough, she agreed to look after the National Trust's half of the Monk Coniston estate as well as her own. 'I have a personal gratification — they have asked me to manage it for them, 'till it is in better order ... interesting work at other people's expense!' So began ten years of intense dialogue with the Trust, during which time — calling herself an amateur land agent — she involved herself in all aspects of management. She was no remote land agent, choosing instead to be involved in selecting tenants, repairing buildings, putting up fences, planting trees and mending walls. And in all matters she put forward firm opinions. 'It's disagreeable to seem to be wiser than other people! But I cannot help saying what I think.'

For farm tenants she appreciated the values of local men, who knew how to gather sheep on the high fells and cope with inclement weather. For applications from 'semi-genteel outsiders', she cautioned that 'it would be desirable to get a very reliable reference. Their morals are sometimes bad or they are people who run debts to tradesmen.' She tried, in selecting tenants and indeed in commenting on their wives, to tread a delicate line between sentimentality and practicality. She was critical of those who did too little in the house: 'there is no getting away from domestic limitations'. On the other hand she was suspicious of those who seemed, in her eyes, to be tidying the place up too much: 'Miss Jackson at Yew Tree is almost too smush. I rather like a genuine farm kitchen, ... [she] has got the house almost too clean ...'

As an outsider, Beatrix could understand the pleasure the Lake District landscape brought to visitors. Even in her late sixties she was writing spontaneously of her delight in it all: 'I was at Buttermere on Friday, ... the valley was as beautiful as a dream — wonderful — spring leaves and gorse in flower.' She did not identify herself with the tourists, and indeed took at times a somewhat superior view, writing

on one occasion 'an undesirable class of day-tripper comes to Coniston village; ... rather a different class visits the Ghyll; fat women off charas, they might fall through the bridge'. Nevertheless she took a business-like approach to their needs for signs, car parks, picnic areas and litter bins. She gently reminded the National Trust that such things as the colour of signs had to be done appropriately. Some sent up from London did not meet with approval: 'On thinking it over it occurred to me that cream and chocolate is likely to be conspicuous in slate country.' She went on to express reservations about the carefully selected Roman lettering, pointing out that there were 'no living Romans left to read it', adding, 'did not someone define good taste as a sense for the fitness of things?'

In hard economic times she realized that the opportunities presented by the ever-increasing number of tourists had to be taken; she was a realistic conservationist and encouraged her tenants to accommodate visitors: 'catering for visitors seems to be the only chance of making farms pay'. At her own expense she set up a small tea-room at Yew Tree Farm, buying up furniture from local sales. 'I have had the luck to meet with a genuine Cumberland dresser, it looks well. And I have hung some watercolours from Lindeth How [on the edge of Windermere, where her mother moved after her father's death] in the meantime to take possession of the walls ... I am so afraid of gifts of rubbish.'

RIGHT *Yew Tree Farm, seen from the Tarn Hows road. Yew Tree is one of the best known of Beatrix's farms, being prominently sited next to the Coniston to Ambleside road. Rising up behind the farm buildings is Holme Fell.*

LEFT ABOVE AND CENTRE *The 'spinning gallery' at Yew Tree Farm, Coniston, drawn by Beatrix on 8 July 1932, and as seen today. Covered galleries such as this are found on several barns and on some houses in and around the edge of the Lake District. Despite their name, there is no evidence for them being used for spinning. The small enclosed room at one end was used to store fleeces.*

LEFT BELOW *Inside Yew Tree Farmhouse.*

Beatrix's purchase of the Monk Coniston estate did not mark the end of her acquisitions. In 1937 she purchased Belmount from Rebecca Owen, who had moved to Rome with her Italian chauffeur. 'The house is scarcely habitable, though it seems a pity to let it fall in — fall *down* it will not. Georgian building stone. Perhaps some time it might be repaired for a hostel ...' Throughout the 1930s and early 1940s she continued to add to her holdings. Although she said often that Troutbeck was her favourite valley, nothing further came up for sale there which she could acquire. She bought four farms in Hawkshead and Little Langdale, and one outlier, Penny Hill Farm, in Eskdale. Apparently she never visited the furthest western valley of Wasdale, and what attracted her to Eskdale is not known. She also purchased cottages to let to local people, understanding only too well that for village communities to continue to flourish craftsmen such as builders and plumbers, as well as farmers, need to be housed. In Near Sawrey she bought six cottages and two more were created from outbuildings. Around Hawkshead, she bought seven in all. In Hawkshead she also helped set up a local association to provide a district nurse for the parishes of Near Sawrey, Hawkshead and Wray, giving to the association a cottage, as well as a car. As Beatrix knew all about the village and people's needs, the first nurse, Nurse Edwards, used to call to see her every day for instructions.

Beatrix managed the Monk Coniston estate for the Trust for almost ten years. From the outset, she had always

LEFT *Belmount, Hawkshead. This grand house, with park-like grounds and views over Esthwaite Water, was the home of Rebecca Owen, who was a Roman Catholic. Beatrix bought the house from her while Rebecca was in Rome in 1937. She never returned, and, after her death, Beatrix had the job of tidying out the place. 'There is her shroud in a cardboard box; presumably blessed by the Pope ... Father Taylor has obligingly buried some unpleasant remains of the early Christians in consecrated ground ...'*

RIGHT *Two views of the porch at Penny Hill Farm, Eskdale.*

Jan 19. 38
Castle Cottage
Sawrey/Ambleside

Dear Bruce Thompson

Mr Heelis has shown me your letter about apportioning rent for Craig House pasture. I agree that it would be much better to have a business arrangement, and I will consult my tenant at High Yewdale. I have never felt any scruple about the use of Craig House, because I have been paying such a very high rent for land belonging to the Trust. This seems a welcome opportunity for adjusting matters.

I remain yrs sincerely
H B Heelis

appreciated that when the Trust had increased its holding sufficiently it would need to appoint a full-time agent. Bruce Thompson was appointed in 1932 and took over from Beatrix six years later. It was perhaps inevitable that her successor would not match her own knowledge and high standards gained through observing the Lake District with an artist's eye for over thirty years.

Despite her appreciation of the situation at one level, it is clear that she could not resist the temptation to judge Bruce Thompson harshly. To say that a certain resentment manifested itself would be an understatement. 'I thought you would have to have an agent sooner or later – but ... I *did hope* he would be a gentleman ... our Westmorland lads are rough; but you have no idea how sharp they are to reckon whether a man is a gentleman or not ... the typical agent has the faults of the idle rich with bumptiousness added.'

Her liaison with Bruce Thompson was an uneasy one. She wrote regularly in forthright fashion to the Trust's secretary in London setting out what she saw as his shortcomings. 'It is useless for me to talk to him. A man cannot help having been born dull. Thompson is supercilious as well.' Her letters were treated with consternation and concern. The Secretary wrote consolingly to Thompson: 'I fully realise ... that none of us are much good in Mrs Heelis' eyes.' Replying to Beatrix, he said: 'The Committee are always glad to hear from you and to have any suggestions from you regarding the better management of the properties of the Trust in the Lake District.' This elicited the rejoinder from Beatrix: 'As regards advice – a man must have judgement to sift the value of advice and advisors, otherwise it is like the fable of the old man and his donkey.'

Despite this particular annoyance with the Trust, generally Beatrix was able to look dispassionately on the organization. Never did her loyalty and support waiver. She continued to give funds, although the full extent of her help is not widely known because several of her donations were made anonymously. She took a long-term view of its problems: 'The Trust is a noble thing and humanly speaking immortal. There are some silly mortals connected with it; but they will pass.'

At the beginning of the Second World War, in 1939, Beatrix was seventy-three years old and by now she was beginning to feel her age. Perhaps she was glad that some of her many responsibilities had been passed on to the Trust. She was quite philosophical about her elder state. 'I do not resent old age; if it brings slowness it brings experience and weight ... to quote a friend, "Thank God I have the seeing eye", that is to say, as I lie in bed I can walk step by step on the fells and rough lands seeing every

stone and flower and patch of bog and cotton grass where my old legs will never take me again. Also do you not feel it is rather pleasing to be so much *wiser* than quantities of young idiots? ... It is a pity the wisdom and experience of old age is largely wasted.'

Nevertheless Beatrix was still a force to be reckoned with. In 1942 she received a phone message inviting her to meet the Minister of Agriculture on the Kirkstone Pass, as he was passing through the Lake District on his way from Scotland to Lancashire. He stopped briefly for ten minutes and she talked to him about hill farming. The following year in June she was invited to take part in 'semi-public work re agricultural committees. You would laugh to see ME in the chair at a meeting of old sheep farmers, discussing prices and subsidies with a young gentleman from the Board of Agriculture.' Government subsidies and the fact that government was buying up all the Herdwick wool for khaki [for soldiers' uniforms] meant hill farmers

LEFT ABOVE *One of the many letters Beatrix wrote to Bruce Thompson, the National Trust's agent in the Lake District. She writes about apportioning rent for a pasture at High Yewdale, one of the farms she kept and managed herself.*

LEFT BELOW *Beatrix judging Herdwick ewes at Keswick Show. In 1943 she was elected president of the Herdwick Sheepbreeders' Association, but did not live long enough to take up the office.*

RIGHT *Hill Top Farm during the Second World War, with temporary silos on the right of the drive. Even upland farms were encouraged to put some land under the plough to help with the war effort.*

LEFT *Beatrix in the porch at Hill Top in the summer of 1943, shortly before her death. Near her feet is a rose of Sharon which still grows around the porch.*

OPPOSITE *A posthumous portait of Beatrix painted around 1950 by her friend Delmar Banner. He depicted what he saw as her 'countenance full of intelligence and humour . . . in which all that is most direct, dignified and engaging in childhood and old age seem to meet'. She is holding a show catalogue and in the background Herdwick sheep are being judged against the backdrop of the Coniston fells.*

FARMING LIFE

were doing reasonably well, but she felt this to be an unsustainable upturn: 'We farmers are apprehensive of what will happen after the war.'

Beatrix was not to see whether her fears about the future of her beloved farming were to be realized, as she died on 22 December that year. She had just signed the conveyances to buy Bank End Cottages and Tower Bank House in Near Sawrey, and, a few days previously, had written her last letter to Anne Carroll Moore: 'surely the war is on the turn. We are enjoying a bright sunny day; snow on the hills. We were lucky to get the hay early here and the oats are not so bad; out a long time but very useful.'

At her funeral a farmer remarked, 'Aye, it's a bad day for farmers.' Afterwards Delmar Banner, her friend, summed up his and his wife Josephine's loss: 'To us, three things seem to mark the end of an age in the Cumbrian dales. One, the flooding of Mardale; one the invasion of the motor; and one the passing of Mrs Heelis.' He also penned this memorable portrait of Beatrix at their first meeting at Castle Cottage in 1935: '... we knocked on the door of her cottage one autumn afternoon. It opened, and we beheld one of her own characters —Mrs Tiggy Winkle perhaps?—yet better than any; short, plump, solid; with apple-red cheeks; and she looked up at us with keen blue eyes and a smile. On her head was a kind of tea cosy, and she was dressed in lots of wool. "Cum in" she said in a snug voice. There was a drugget on the floor, and silver mounted guns on the walls. In the room into which we followed her bent and venerable figure there was a cheerful fire. She sat down on a red plush armchair on one side, we sat on stiff-backed chairs on the other. She took us in; and during the searching silence we neither spoke nor moved. We noticed a fine Girtin on the wall; her husband's

slippers on the fender; and (for her age) a rather naughty quantity of silver chocolate-paper on a little table.'

In her will, Beatrix left 4,049 acres of land to the National Trust including fourteen farms and twenty houses. She specified that Hill Top should not be let to a tenant and that the rooms should remain as she left them. On her farms, the landlord's flocks were to be maintained as pure Herdwick. This legacy remains one of the largest and most significant ever made to the organization, 'a world of beauty that will survive'.

Epilogue

William Heelis survived his wife for barely two years. Without her company he pined away. Under the terms of Beatrix's will, all her property which she bequeathed to the National Trust was passed to her husband for his lifetime, apart from Belmount which was left directly to him. He was to decide which parts were to be handed over immediately. In the event he chose to keep none of it, including Belmount.

In his own will, he left all his property to the Trust. This included three farms and three cottages and also his solicitors' office in Hawkshead, now the Beatrix Potter Gallery.

Winter at Moss Eccles Tarn, where Beatrix and William kept a boat. 'William and I fished (at least I rowed) till darkness; coming down the lane about eleven. It was lovely on the tarn, not a breath of wind . . . '

Beatrix Potter: Short Biography

Unless otherwise stated, all books were originally published in London by Frederick Warne. In addition, the list below does not include twenty-one pieces of land also purchased by Beatrix between 1905 and 1940.

1866 Born on 28 July at Bolton Gardens, London

1882 First visit to the Lake District; stays at Wray Castle

1901 *The Tale of Peter Rabbit* printed privately

1902 *The Tale of Peter Rabbit* published by Frederick Warne, who became her publisher

1903 *The Tale of Squirrel Nutkin, The Tailor of Gloucester*

1904 *The Tale of Benjamin Bunny, The Tale of Two Bad Mice*

1905 *The Tale of The Pie and The Patty-Pan*
Engaged to Norman Warne
Norman Warne dies
Buys Hill Top Farm, Near Sawrey

1906 *The Tale of Mr. Jeremy Fisher, The Story of A Fierce Bad Rabbit, The Story of Miss Moppet*

1907 *The Tale of Tom Kitten*

1908 *The Tale of Jemima Puddle-Duck, The Tale of Samuel Whiskers*

1909 *The Tale of Ginger and Pickles, The Tale of The Flopsy Bunnies*
Buys Castle Farm and the Castle, Near Sawrey

1910 *The Tale of Mrs. Tittlemouse*

1911 *The Tale of Timmy Tiptoes*

1912 *The Tale of Mr. Tod*

1913 *The Tale of Pigling Bland*
Marries William Heelis on 17 October and moves to Castle Cottage

1915 Buys Courier Cottage, Near Sawrey

1917 *Appley Dapply's Nursery Rhymes*
Buys three houses at Hawkshead Fields, Hawkshead

1918 *The Tale of Johnny Town-Mouse*

1922 *Cecily Parsley's Nursery Rhymes*

1923 Buys Troutbeck Park Farm, Troutbeck

1925 Buys Thimble Hall and the Corner Shop, Hawkshead

1929 *The Fairy Caravan* printed privately and in Philadelphia

1930 *The Tale of Little Pig Robinson*, also printed in Philadelphia
Buys Monk Coniston Estate, Coniston. Transfers at cost to the National Trust: High Tilberthwaite Farm, Low Hallgarth Farm and two cottages, Low Tilberthwaite Farm and Cottages, Yew Tree Farm, Tarn Hows, Rose Castle. Gives to the National Trust: Holme Ground Farm. Keeps: Far End Farm, High Oxenfell Farm, High Park Farm, High Yewdale Farm, Low Yewdale Farm, Stang End Farm, Waterhead Cottages

1932 *Sister Anne* published in Philadelphia

1933 Buys Low Greengate and the Old Post Office, Near Sawrey

1934 Buys Bridge End Farm, Little Langdale

1935 Buys Penny Hill Farm, Eskdale, and Busk Farm, Little Langdale

1936 Buys Dale End Farm and Brow Cottage, Little Langdale, and Low Oxenfell Farm, Coniston

1937 Buys Belmount, Hawkshead

1943 Buys Black Beck Lodge and Cottage, Hawkshead, and High and Low Loanthwaite Farms, Hawkshead

1943 Dies on 22 December at Castle Cottage. Cremated in Blackpool on 31 December. Her ashes scattered somewhere on the fells above Near Sawrey

1944 Her purchase of Tower Bank House and two cottages at Bank End, Near Sawrey, completed and the properties conveyed directly to the National Trust
Wag-by-Wall and *The Horn Book* published in Boston

1944 All her property conveyed to the National Trust in June under the terms of her will

1945 William Heelis dies on 4 August

1947 William Heelis's property conveyed to the National Trust under the terms of his will: Bend-or-Bump Cottage and the Solicitors' Office, Hawkshead, High Tock How Farm, Tock How Cottages, Hole Farm and High Wray Farm, Wray

Map of Beatrix Potter's Lake District

The map opposite shows some of the principal places relevant to Beatrix Potter's life in the Lake District and property purchased by her.

land

houses

farms

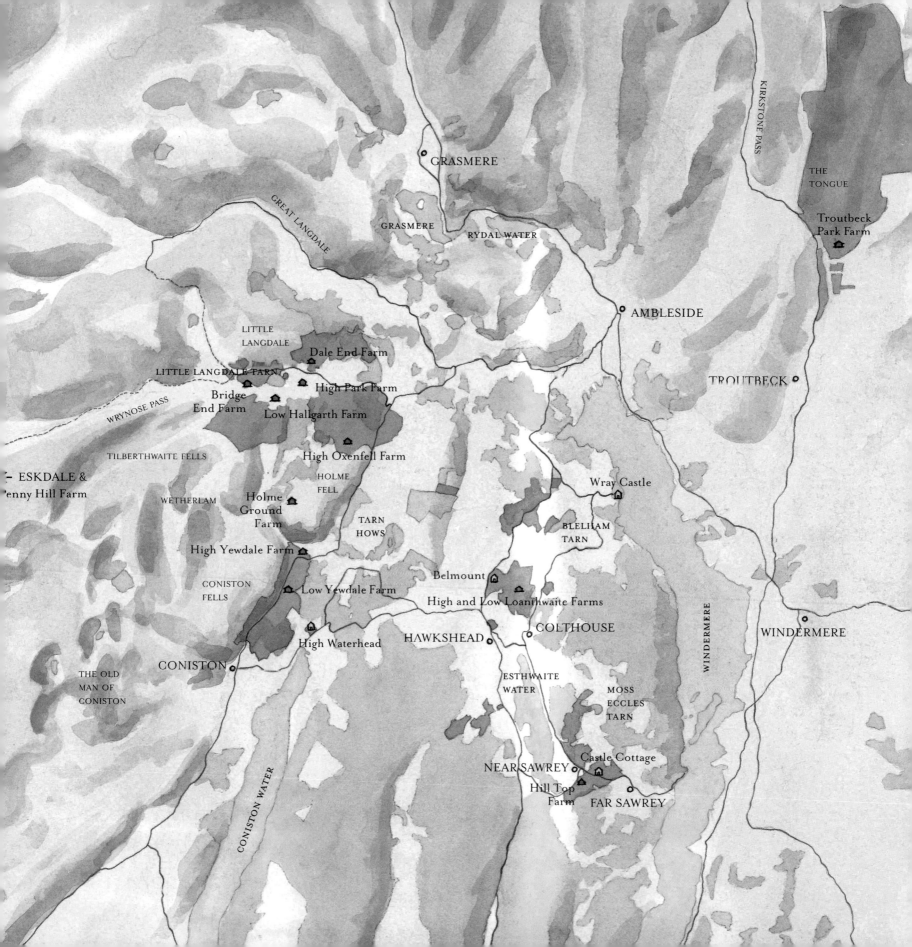

GRASMERE

GRASMERE

RYDAL WATER

KIRKSTONE PASS

THE TONGUE

Troutbeck Park Farm

GREAT LANGDALE

AMBLESIDE

LITTLE LANGDALE

Dale End Farm

TROUTBECK

LITTLE LANGDALE TARN

High Park Farm

Bridge End Farm

Low Hallgarth Farm

WRYNOSE PASS

TILBERTHWAITE FELLS

High Oxenfell Farm

HOLME FELL

Wray Castle

– ESKDALE &
'enny Hill Farm

WETHERLAM

Holme Ground Farm

TARN HOWS

BLELHAM TARN

WINDERMERE

High Yewdale Farm

Belmount

CONISTON FELLS

Low Yewdale Farm

High and Low Loanthwaite Farms

COLTHOUSE

WINDERMERE

THE OLD MAN OF CONISTON

High Waterhead

HAWKSHEAD

ESTHWAITE WATER

MOSS ECCLES TARN

CONISTON

Castle Cottage

NEAR SAWREY

Hill Top Farm

FAR SAWREY

CONISTON WATER

Index

NOTE: Page numbers in *italic* refer to captions to the illustrations.

Select Bibliography

ON BEATRIX POTTER

Davies, Hunter, *Beatrix Potter's Lakeland*, revised edition, Frederick
Warne, London and New York, 1999

Denyer, Susan, 'Beatrix Potter and the Monk Coniston Estate',
in *Beatrix Potter and Mrs Heelis*, Beatrix Potter Studies IV, 1990

Denyer, Susan, *Beatrix Potter and Her Farms*, National Trust,
London, 1992

Denyer, Susan, '"This Quixotic Venture": Beatrix Potter and
the National Trust', in Taylor, J. (ed) *So I Shall Tell You a Story*,
Frederick Warne, London and New York, 1993

Denyer, Susan, 'Beatrix Potter and the Decorative Arts', in
Beatrix Potter and the Lake District, Beatrix Potter Studies VII, 1996

Heelis, John, *The Tale of Mrs William Heelis, Beatrix Potter*, Sutton
Publishing, Stroud, 1999

Hobbs, Anne Stevenson, *Beatrix Potter's Art*, Frederick Warne,
London and New York, 1990

Linder, Leslie, *The Journal of Beatrix Potter*, revised edition,
Frederick Warne, London and New York, 1989

Taylor, Judy, *Beatrix Potter's Letters*, Frederick Warne, London and
New York, 1992

Taylor, Judy, *Beatrix Potter, Artist, Storyteller and Countrywoman*,
Frederick Warne, London and New York, 1996

Taylor, Judy, *Beatrix Potter and Hill Top*, revised edition, National
Trust, London, 1998

Taylor, Judy, Whalley, Irene, Hobbs, Anne Stevenson and
Battrick, Elizabeth, *Beatrix Potter 1866–1943: The Artist and her
World*, Frederick Warne and the National Trust, London and
New York, 1987

ON THE LAKE DISTRICT

Denyer, Susan, *Traditional Buildings and Life in the Lake District*, Victor
Gollancz, 1992

Denyer, Susan, *Herdwick Sheep Farming*, National Trust, 1993

Denyer, Susan, *Lake District Landscapes*, National Trust, 1994

Denyer, Susan, and Martin, Janet, *A Century in the Lake District*,
National Trust, 1995

Rollinson, William, *Life and Tradition in the Lake District*, revised
edition, Dalesman Books, Clapham, 1995

AUTHOR'S ACKNOWLEDGMENTS

I have quoted heavily from Beatrix's own words. These have come from a variety of sources, including:

Letters written to the National Trust between 1926 and 1943
Letters to her American friends, collected and published by
  Jane Cromwell Morse in *Beatrix Potter's Americans: Selected Letters*,
  The Horn Book, Inc., Boston, 1982
Letters to friends and relations, collected and published by Judy Taylor
  in *Beatrix Potter's Letters*, Frederick Warne, London and New York, 1992
Letters collected and published as quotes by Margaret Lane in *The Magic
  Years of Beatrix Potter*, Frederick Warne, London and New York, 1978,
  and *The Tale of Beatrix Potter*, Frederick Warne, London and New York,
  1946
Instructions on possessions at Hill Top, mostly marked on individual
  items
Beatrix's Journal, transcribed and published by Leslie Linder in
  The Journal of Beatrix Potter, revised edition, Frederick Warne,
  London, 1989

Many people have contributed in a variety of ways to this book and I would particularly like to pay tribute to the following: Sally Floyer at Frederick Warne; Anne Stevenson Hobbs and Paul Harrison of the Victoria and Albert Museum; the staff, both present and past, at Hill Top and the Beatrix Potter Gallery, in particular Mike Hemmings and Catherine Pritchard; tenants, both past and present, of Beatrix's farms; all those, alive and dead, who have added to the sum total of our knowledge of Beatrix through recounting and recording their memories of her – in particular, Tom Storey, Willow Taylor, Josephine Banner, John Heelis, David Beckett; Janet Martin; Elizabeth Battrick; Margaret Willes of the National Trust; Frances Lincoln and the editorial and design staff at Frances Lincoln Ltd.

Naturally, however, I take responsibility for what appears here; the views expressed are entirely my own and are not necessarily those of the National Trust.

PUBLISHERS' ACKNOWLEDGMENTS

The publishers would like to thank Nicola Saunders at Frederick Warne for all her help with the archive photographs and drawings and Marie Lorimer for compiling the index and proofreading.

PICTURE ACKNOWLEDGMENTS

Listed by page number. **a** = above **b** = below **c** = centre **l** = left **r** = right

PHOTOGRAPHS
Joe Cornish 16–17; 23; 27; 29b; 34–5; 46–7; 105–7; 109a & b; 110–11; 114–7; 120–1; 122b; 127–9; 130–2; 138–9.
Stephen Robson 86–7; 90–1; 92–3; 95l; 96–7; 99 the National Trust Photographic Library; 100–3.
Simon Upton 1; 5; 24; 30–3; 36–7; 40b; 42–4; 49–50; 52; 55–7; 58l; 58–9; 60–1; 62b–64; 66–7; 68–9; 71–6; 77 ar & br; 78–81; 82–4; 85 ar & br; 123b; 130cl; 130 bl; 133.

ARCHIVE PHOTOGRAPHS AND DRAWINGS
Reproduced by kind permission of Frederick Warne & Co.
2–3 Copyright © F. Warne & Co. 1922, Courtesy of the National Trust; 4 Courtesy of the National Trust; 61 Copyright © F. Warne & Co. 1978; 6–7 Courtesy of the Victoria and Albert Museum; 8 Courtesy of the National Trust; 9 Copyright © F. Warne & Co. 1972; 10a Copyright © F. Warne & Co. 1972; 10b Copyright © F. Warne & Co. 1955; 11 Courtesy of the Victoria and Albert Museum; 12 Copyright © F. Warne & Co. 1955; 13l Copyright © F. Warne & Co. 1966; 13r Copyright © F. Warne & Co. 1955; 14 Courtesy of private collector; 15 Courtesy of the National Trust; 18 Courtesy of private collector; 19l Copyright © F. Warne & Co. 1955; 19r Copyright © F. Warne & Co.; 20 Copyright © F. Warne & Co. 1946, Courtesy of the Frederick Warne Archive; 21a Courtesy of the National Trust; 21b Copyright © F. Warne & Co.; 22 Courtesy of the National Trust; 25 Copyright © F. Warne & Co. 1955; 26 Copyright © F. Warne & Co. 1978; 28 Courtesy of the National Trust; 29a Copyright © F. Warne & Co. 1992, Courtesy of the National Trust; 30l Copyright © F. Warne & Co.; 34al Courtesy of private collector; 34bl Courtesy of the Victoria and Albert Museum; 38 Copyright © F. Warne & Co. 1955; 39 Copyright © F. Warne & Co. 1985; 40al Courtesy of the Victoria and Albert Museum; 40ar Courtesy of the Victoria and Albert Museum; 41 Copyright © F. Warne & Co.; 45 Courtesy of the National Trust; 48l Courtesy of the Victoria and Albert Museum; 48r Copyright © F. Warne & Co. 1908, 1987; 51 Copyright © F. Warne & Co. 1908, 1987; 53 Copyright © F. Warne & Co.; 54 Copyright © F. Warne & Co. 1908, 1987; 62a Copyright © F. Warne & Co. 1955; 65 Copyright © F. Warne & Co. 1908, 1987; 67r Copyright © F. Warne & Co. 1908, 1987; 70 Copyright © F. Warne & Co. 1904, 1987; 77l Copyright © F. Warne & Co. 1904, 1987; 82l Courtesy of the Victoria and Albert Museum; 85l Copyright © F. Warne & Co. 1908, 1987; 87r Copyright © F. Warne & Co. 1907, 1987; 88l Copyright © F. Warne & Co. 1955; 88r Copyright © F. Warne & Co.; 89 Courtesy of the National Trust; 91r Copyright © F. Warne & Co. 1908, 1987; 94 Courtesy of the National Trust; 95r Courtesy of the National Trust; 98 Courtesy of the National Trust; 100l Copyright © F. Warne & Co. 1907, 1987; 104 Copyright © F. Warne & Co. 1978; 108l Copyright © F. Warne & Co. 1955; 109c Copyright © F. Warne & Co. 1985; 111r Copyright © F. Warne & Co. 1906, 1987; 112 Copyright © F. Warne & Co. 1908, 1987; 113a Copyright © F. Warne & Co. 1955; 113b Copyright © F. Warne & Co. 1912, 1987; 114l Copyright © F. Warne & Co. 1913; 117r Copyright © F. Warne & Co. 1908, 1987; 118 Courtesy of the National Trust; 119 Copyright © F. Warne & Co., Courtesy of the National Trust; 122a Copyright © F. Warne & Co. 1998; 123a Courtesy of the National Trust; 124 Copyright © F. Warne & Co. 1929; 125 Copyright © F. Warne & Co. 1917, 1987; 126 Copyright © F. Warne & Co.; 130al Courtesy of the National Trust; 134a Copyright © F. Warne & Co.; 134b Courtesy of private collector; 135 Courtesy of the National Trust; 136 By permission of Frederick Warne & Co.; 137 Copyright © F. Warne & Co. 1966, Courtesy of the National Portrait Gallery.

MAP
141 Joanna Logan. Copyright © Frances Lincoln 2000.